Cambridge English Readers

Level 6

Series editor: Philip

Frozen Pizza
and other slices of life

Antoinette Moses

CAMBRIDGE
UNIVERSITY PRESS

CAMBRIDGE
UNIVERSITY PRESS

University Printing House, Cambridge CB2 8BS, United Kingdom

Cambridge University Press is part of the University of Cambridge.

It furthers the University's mission by disseminating knowledge in the pursuit of education, learning and research at the highest international levels of excellence.

www.cambridge.org
Information on this title: www.cambridge.org/9780521750783

© Cambridge University Press 2002

First published 2002
Reprinted 2016

Printed in the United Kingdom by Hobbs the Printers Ltd

A catalogue record for this publication is available from the British Library

ISBN 978-0-521-75078-3 Paperback

Contents

Two Worlds

'I'm not taking my car! Not near that estate! The kids will steal it or steal the wheels off it! I only bought it a month ago! What if . . . ?'

'OK, OK,' Karen interrupted quickly. 'You've made your point, John. You don't have to take your new car on the film shoot tomorrow.'

She sighed to herself. John was a good cameraman, but he wasn't the easiest man to work with.

'Just hire a car big enough for the three of us and all your equipment. And let me get on with my work,' she added. It wasn't easy being a woman director, she reflected. Sometimes you had to be tough or your team wouldn't take you seriously. Unfortunately John had worked with her for too many years and knew Karen far too well. She could be tough, she had to be sometimes. But for the people who worked for her, she would do anything. That was what they said when she wasn't listening. John didn't even pretend to be upset when she got cross with him.

'Do we get danger money?' he began again. 'I've heard that . . .'

'Out!' commanded Karen.

'But . . .'

'John, get out of my office right now before I . . .'

'But I was only . . .' John started again.

'Get out before I throw something!'

John left and Karen turned back to her computer and her preparations for the following day's filming.

The idea for the series had come to her while she was reading the newspapers one morning. There were a lot of articles about children in England. Compared with other European countries it didn't do very well. Too many children lived in poverty. The figures shocked her. She herself didn't know anyone who could really be called poor and she was sure that most of her friends didn't either. It was as if there were two different Englands living side by side. She knew immediately that she wanted to make a documentary series about this. She had sat up all that night and written an outline and the next morning she went straight to Adrian, her producer.

'Yes,' he had said. 'I like it.' This was one of the many things that Karen liked about working for Adrian. He made immediate decisions and said what he thought.

'One nation, but divided into the haves and the have-nots. I think it's the right time to do a whole series on England's forgotten children. Of course you will want to include the north–south divide?'

Karen nodded. This was the way most people thought that England was divided. The north of England was where all the poor people lived and the south was the rich part of the country. She knew that it wasn't that simple, but it was what people thought. No, she corrected herself, it was what some people who lived in the south thought. Reasonably wealthy people living in the south. People like Adrian and herself.

'Yes,' she answered. 'I think we have to.'

'The prime minister says the divide doesn't exist any more,' Adrian reminded her. 'Haven't you read about how England has changed? There are more millionaires in the north of England than in the south.'

'Yes,' Karen sighed. 'I've read all about that. I know that in Leeds there's now a branch of Harvey Nichols where people can buy all the same designer clothes that were only available in London before. But Leeds is only one northern city. There's still more unemployment in the north of England than in the south. Most of the best-paid jobs are in the south and most head offices are down here, in or around London. And house prices are much higher in the south. There is still a divide, whatever the prime minister says.'

'I agree with you.' Adrian smiled. 'But at the same time I think that a lot of the differences between the south and the north are simply to do with how we see people.' He frowned.

'What do you mean?' asked Karen.

'Well,' began Adrian, 'look at Linda, for example.'

Linda worked for their TV production company as a researcher. It was she who went out and found the right people to interview. She conducted her own interviews, which she gave to Karen, so that Karen knew before they did any filming who was likely to say what.

'Just because Linda comes from Manchester and has a northern accent, people here in London think that she must be stupid,' continued Adrian. 'In fact she got a first-class degree at Cambridge University, she knows more about economics than I'll ever know and she's the best researcher we've ever had here. But there's always some idiot making jokes about pie and chips, as if that's all people from Manchester eat.'

'I know.' Karen said. Karen liked Linda and they sometimes went out for a drink or a meal together after work. Linda often complained about the very thing that Adrian was talking about.

'Everyone thinks I'm stupid because I have a Manchester accent,' she had told Karen. 'But I'm not changing the way I speak for any insensitive Londoners; I can tell you that right now!'

Karen smiled at Adrian as she remembered the conversation. She was fascinated by the way that Adrian seemed to care about Linda. Was there something going on between him and Linda that she didn't know about, Karen wondered.

That conversation with Adrian had been two months ago. And Adrian had not only liked her idea, but had rung up the head of documentaries at the network the same day. And only two weeks later he'd persuaded the network that it was just what they wanted right now. Karen had never known an idea for a documentary series go through the system so fast. It usually took months and months, and sometimes years. But the network had been criticised recently for not having enough serious programmes, and they had decided to cancel a new series on people with unusual hobbies. That had left a gap in the autumn programming and this new series would fill it nicely.

'So, here I am,' thought Karen, looking at the computer, 'with a six-part series to produce, very little time and too much to do. As usual.' Filming was starting the next day and she still had only a rough idea of how she wanted to tell her story. She had written outlines and draft scripts, but there were still a lot of gaps.

'I think we should start close to home,' she had told Adrian. 'Home in the sense of the office,' she added.

Their company had a floor in Canary Wharf. Everyone called it Canary Wharf, but its proper name was Number 1, Canada Square. It was the tallest building in England, although Karen thought that it would not be long before someone built a taller one. She liked working there. It was a building that everyone knew. You could see it from miles away, a huge tower, fifty-two storeys high. Several newspapers had offices in the tower, and occasionally a friend of Karen's who worked for one of them would let her use their files to help her research her stories. It saved her hours of work and trips to the library.

But with this new series there was no need to go to the library or visit her friend at the newspaper. All the information she wanted was recent and that meant that all the facts Karen needed were on the Internet. It took her just two days to get all the facts she needed to write the background pieces. She would use these as the voice-over material.

The film would show views of the different places, while an actor's voice reported all the facts. Then they would cut to the interviews.

Karen still hadn't decided which actor to use for the voice-overs. That was her next job today. She had to listen to some tapes and decide which actor to choose to read the voice-overs. It was so important to get the right voice. You didn't want any of the report to sound like a boring lesson at school. You didn't want people to switch off or change channels. So you had to choose a good clear but friendly voice.

It wasn't easy, but she had plenty of choice. There were so many good actors around, and most of them were perfectly happy to do voice-over work for documentaries, especially on a series like this one. Many of them had kids themselves. They cared about children.

Karen made a decision and then began to make notes for tomorrow's shoot. They were going to interview this kid, what was her name? Rosie. Karen read through the interview Linda had done with Rosie and underlined the bits that she thought were important. These were the things she wanted the girl to say when they filmed her.

'Poor kid,' Karen thought, reading Linda's outline on Rosie's background. Rosie lived on a housing estate only half a mile from her office, but it was a world away from Karen's London.

She looked out of the window and thought about how easy her life was. If she didn't go straight home to the flat she shared with two friends from university, there were plenty of other things to do. She could take a boat from Canary Wharf along the Thames and then visit the new Tate Modern. This gallery of contemporary art, housed in the huge old power station at Bankside, was one of the most exciting places that Karen knew. In fact that whole area of the Thames was so exciting now, she thought. There was the new Globe Theatre, an almost exact copy of Shakespeare's old theatre, where the audience stood and took part in the productions as they had in Shakespeare's day. There was the National Theatre and the concert halls and the film theatre and festivals and free poetry events – all the things that made living in London such fun.

It wasn't a world that the kids on Rosie's estate knew. Karen read Linda's notes. Some of the children didn't go to school. They sometimes went in the morning to have their names ticked, and then left as soon as they could. Getting their names ticked made life easier, the children had told Linda. It meant that no one was looking for them.

'But why don't you stay at school?' Linda had asked them.

'There's no point, is there?' they had replied.

'No point?' she had repeated.

'No,' they told her. There was no reason to go to school because they couldn't see any point in an education. They only saw life on their housing estate, where a lot of the men were out of work.

'Why bother going to school?' Rosie herself had asked. 'What's the point?'

'It's awful,' Linda commented to Karen after she had got back from her research trip. 'These kids just can't imagine any kind of life outside the estate. If something isn't done about them, they'll become a lost generation of children.'

'Yes,' said Karen. 'And what makes it really horrifying is that these children live so near here. The London we know doesn't exist for these kids, does it? We just can't imagine what life must be like on an estate like that.'

'No,' Linda agreed. 'I thought I knew what it would be like there. I've seen places like that on television, in documentaries and in plays and films. But it's the smell. That never comes over on television. All the flats smell of damp and old meals. But it's not just actual smells, which are bad enough, but the smell of hopelessness. I can't describe it any other way. I don't know how you can catch it on film.'

'Nor do I,' Karen replied, thoughtfully.

There were two worlds, she was thinking, her world and the world that these children lived in. A world of damp houses, of being hungry and bored. A world where violence was never far away. A world where some children couldn't even read or write and none of them thought that things would get better.

*   *   *

The next day was sunny and Rosie woke up as usual to the sound of her little sister, Kylie, crying. Her mother shouted something but didn't get up. Rosie knew that she had been drinking the previous night and probably wouldn't get up until lunchtime. Rosie swung her thin legs over the bed and walked on bare feet across the room, where she and her sister slept, to the kitchen. It was dirty as usual and the floor felt sticky under her feet. She opened the fridge, took out a bottle of milk and smelt it. Luckily, for once it smelt OK, and there was even a packet of cornflakes. Rosie poured some of the breakfast cereal into the bowl, added some milk and put it on the table. Kylie was three, but she had problems talking. Social services wanted her to go to a special school, but her mum refused. She was scared that she would never see her daughter again.

'It's not like that, Mary,' the social services had told her mother. 'Kylie will come home for the holidays.' But Rosie's mum still refused, and the social workers couldn't force her. They came round quite often to check on Rosie and Kylie, but there wasn't a lot they could do. Rosie always said that she went to school and she did go in briefly once or twice a week. Then she'd go and meet the other kids on the estate or go back to the flat and look after Kylie.

'You kids, you're all I've got,' her mum would say whenever she was sober and often when she was drunk. It was true, Rosie thought. Rosie looked after her sister and made sure that her mum didn't fall asleep with a cigarette in her hand. And her mum did love her and Kylie. In her own way.

Kylie ate her cornflakes and Rosie wiped her face afterwards with a bit of a towel that wasn't too dirty. There was even enough milk and cornflakes for her, too. It was going to be a good day, she decided. Perhaps she'd go to town on the buses today.

It was one of the few times she and her friends left the estate. Going on the buses meant that you jumped on a bus, usually during the crowded time of day when people were going to work. Then you went upstairs and stayed on as long as you could before the conductor came round and asked for your money. When that happened, you pretended you'd lost your money and ran downstairs and jumped off the bus. You couldn't do it on the new buses where the driver took the fares, but only on the old double-decker buses where there was both a driver and a conductor. Some days you could get all the way into the centre of London before the conductor bothered to come upstairs to check travel cards and collect money for tickets. Other days you were spotted as you got on by a conductor who knew you and then you had to get off quickly before they called the police. Getting home was always harder and sometimes you had to get lots of different buses. And sometimes you had to walk half the way home.

Yes, thought Rosie, she'd go on the buses today. She could go as far as Regent's Park, and then she might even be able to persuade someone that she'd lost her pocket money and get them to pay for the entrance to London Zoo. Rosie loved the zoo. She could look at the animals all day and people often didn't finish their meals at the cafés. She found crisps, chips, half-finished ice cream and once a whole hamburger that someone had ordered but not eaten.

All her life Rosie had been hungry. Not badly hungry, just a feeling that she wanted more. When she did stay at school she got a free lunch and could eat as much as she liked, but that meant lessons. It wasn't that she was stupid. When she was younger she had been near the top of her class. She just couldn't see why she should learn things. And someone had to look after Kylie. 'What's the point?' she always said. 'What's the point of school?' she'd said to that researcher woman the other day.

Rosie jumped off her chair. It was Wednesday. That meant that today was the day that they were coming to film the estate.

'That'll be a laugh,' Rosie's friend Bryan had said. 'Perhaps we can steal the wheels off their van while they're filming.' 'Or get a camera,' said an older boy. 'You can get a lot of money for a camera.'

'No,' said Rosie. 'No-one's going to buy a camera off us, they'd know it was stolen.'

'Yeah,' a boy called Pete agreed. 'And that film woman

Linda said they would pay us to watch the van and make sure that nothing walked.'

'They've been here before then!' Rosie laughed. 'They know what to do.'

She didn't tell her friends that Linda had chosen her. She thought they'd laugh at her. Anyway, Rosie decided, the film people had probably changed their minds by now. People never did what they promised.

But it seemed that they hadn't changed their minds. And they were subtle about the way they went off with Rosie. They asked to see Kylie and then it was natural for Rosie to take them to her flat. Karen had been shocked by the state of Rosie's flat and just couldn't bear the thought of being shut up there for a few hours' filming. But Rosie herself was great. She was so natural and bright.

'Do you know why they call this a sink estate?' she asked Karen.

'No,' Karen replied. 'Do you?'

'It's because we can't sink down any further,' Rosie laughed. Then she thought for a moment. 'Or because they've pulled the plug on us like we're just dirty bath water and they're letting us go down the plughole.'

'That's a good definition,' Linda whispered to Karen.

Rosie's mum was awake but hadn't got dressed, so Karen suggested that they take a boat trip.

'Do you like going on the river?' Karen asked Rosie.

'I've never been,' Rosie replied. 'You'd never be able to get on those boats for free,' she thought.

Anyhow she'd never liked going near the River Thames. It was where, when you were small, the bigger boys had threatened to throw you in. Where you went when the tide was low to see if you could find old coins or anything else that you could sell.

But you didn't often go near the river because it was dirty and cold and there was enough dirt and cold in your life already.

'We could go to Tate Modern,' suggested Karen. 'We could go round the gallery and then have a meal in a café. Is that OK?'

'Yeah, why not?' said Rosie. Food was always OK, she thought. She didn't like the sound of the gallery bit, but she was hungry and you never got anything for nothing.

They couldn't film inside the gallery, so the film crew waited outside, setting up the camera for the interview, and Karen and Rosie went round the exhibitions.

'Wow! You could get the whole estate in here,' Rosie announced as they entered the huge entrance hall.

Karen had not been sure how Rosie would react to the gallery. She pointed out how the exhibitions were arranged according to subject – memory, the environment, real life. Rosie, however, had her own way of looking at the artworks. The lobster on the telephone made her laugh, but she said that she thought it was silly.

'I like these though,' Rosie said as they walked into the Mark Rothko room. Karen herself found the red and black paintings rather difficult. 'I could sit here all day,' said Rosie. 'It's like just before you go to sleep,' she added. 'You feel safe.'

Rosie liked the Henry Moore sculptures, too. 'You see that one,' said Rosie, pointing to a figure of a woman lying down. 'It makes me think of my mum. It looks all solid on the outside but there's a big hole in the middle.'

Karen nodded. She was amazed at Rosie's responses.

'I'm glad you like it,' she said.

'Yeah,' agreed Rosie. 'I didn't expect to like it. I thought it would be really boring. But it isn't. It's even better than the zoo. And it isn't as cold,' she added.

'You can come here any time you like,' Karen told her.

'I can't. I don't have the money,' explained Rosie.

'No, it's free,' Karen told her.

'And no-one would chase me out?'

'No. No-one.'

Rosie thought about this for a moment and then nodded. They walked round some of the other rooms and then went outside where the film crew was waiting.

Rosie's interview was perfect. Karen knew that the people watching the programme would be affected by Rosie and her story. Perhaps it would even bring the estate some money, thought Karen. Perhaps it might help. It was what she always hoped.

After the interview Rosie asked if she could go back inside the gallery.

'Of course,' said Karen.

Rosie walked back inside. It was true. No-one stopped her. No-one objected. She felt very small inside the huge space, but at the same time, strangely free.

It would be her secret, thought Rosie, her special place, her new world.

The Old Oak Bowl

Water is clear, but when there is a great mass of it, it is clear no longer. Stand behind a great waterfall and you can watch the falling water, but you cannot see through it. Things are not always what you believe them to be.

Robert Walker believed that life was simple. He knew who he was and what he did. He was an Englishman, a schoolteacher and a woodworker. This was the subject he taught at a small public school and had taught there for forty years. The school had once been a well-respected boys' school, but in the 1980s it had begun to admit girls. Mr Walker (nobody ever called him Robert) had been against the change, but now found that some girls were rather good at woodwork. He had also discovered that the boys behaved better when there were girls in the class. Nevertheless, he still complained about the change and told new teachers how much better the school had been in the old days.

New teachers very quickly learned to ignore Mr Walker.

'Don't take any notice of the old boy,' said Greg Mount, the history teacher. 'Walker talks rubbish, but he knows everything there is to know about working in wood. The kids love his classes. They just think he's a dinosaur.'

'They all think I'm a dinosaur,' thought Mr Walker. 'But at least I know who I am and what it is I believe in. These days young people don't know what to believe in.' And on

Sundays he went to the local church and thanked God that he was an Englishman and still had his health and a good job and knew what was right.

Mr Walker knew exactly what was right and what was wrong. It was right that woods and forests were looked after properly so that good trees could grow and that dead or dying trees were cut down. It was right to open doors for ladies and to say 'please' and 'thank you' at all times. It was right to tell the truth, even if people didn't always want to hear it.

It was wrong, Mr Walker believed, to think that new meant good and old meant bad. It was wrong to make too many changes and to try to run before you could walk. And it was wrong to allow too many foreigners into England.

It seemed to Mr Walker that there were too many foreigners at the school these days. He only called them foreigners to himself, as the other teachers said they were English, part of the new multicultural society. But despite the fact they all spoke English, Mr Walker could not help feeling that they weren't really English. Their families hadn't always lived in England and many of them were coloured. He had learned not to use that word in public, but he could not help saying it to himself. He disliked the term 'black'; he thought 'coloured' was more suitable.

Mr Walker thought that things had been much simpler in the old days when England was England and . . . well . . . the English were English. It wasn't right to mix things up. And it wasn't just the students. Mr Walker had found an English textbook which was full of examples of Caribbean poetry. One poem was about 'mugging de

Queen's English'. Mr Walker was deeply shocked by this and took the book to the headteacher. But it seemed that this poet, John Agard, was famous and everybody accepted his poems.

'Well really!' said Mr Walker to himself as he walked back to the small cottage where he lived. 'I'm glad that there aren't any changes like that in woodworking.'

Mr Walker had been living in this same cottage ever since he came to the school. He did not need much room as he ate most of his meals in the school. So he had turned the old cottage kitchen into a place where he could work on his own projects. When he was not working, he would sit in his front room and read history books. He liked to read about the history of England and all the great battles.

The past showed you the way forward, he thought. You could always learn from history. He read many books about Elizabeth I. England was at its best in the sixteenth and seventeenth centuries, he thought. Even though it became stronger and more powerful later, this was the period when England was really great. Mr Walker often told Greg Mount this. He knew that Greg did not agree with him. Greg liked all the changes and the new ideas. Mr Walker knew that Greg would never agree with him. But he knew he was right all the same.

Whenever he was not teaching or reading, Mr Walker would work, mending and restoring old furniture. He knew how to mend wooden furniture. It was very satisfying. Mr Walker believed that old things deserved respect. It was not right to throw them away and buy new things. Almost any good old chair could be restored and made new again. It took a lot of time, but he was not in a hurry. The chairs he mended filled his house and those of his colleagues. He never charged them more than the cost of the materials, although he knew that the chairs were now worth considerably more. His colleagues knew it, too, but only one of them had ever sold one of his chairs to a London antique shop. She had made a couple of hundred pounds profit from it, but Mr Walker thought it was wrong for her to do so. It was not that he felt that she should have given him the money. No. It was the fact that she had sold what was almost a present. It was not right to sell presents.

At weekends Mr Walker would get into his old van, which he had had for so many years that it was now itself an antique, and drive to the local antique shops. The owners knew him, and if they found any old furniture that looked as if it should be thrown away, they would often keep it for him.

He would not, however, restore furniture for them to sell in their shops.

'I'm a teacher; I don't buy and sell antiques,' he always remarked. 'Maybe one day when I retire I might take up that kind of work, but until then it's just my little hobby.' Since Mr Walker was clearly already over seventy years old – the school had made a special case for keeping him after retirement age – no-one thought that he was ever going to retire. But Mr Walker would, very occasionally, mend a special piece of furniture for a shop, just because he could not bear to see good furniture in a bad state.

One Saturday Mr Walker arrived at a small antique shop, just off the High Street, with a small eighteenth century table which he had just restored. It was a circular table and when Mr Walker lifted it out of his van, the wood shone like a mirror.

'Mr Walker!' exclaimed the large, red-haired woman who owned the shop. Mr Walker thought she coloured her hair, but did not let that upset him too much as she often found excellent pieces of furniture. 'Mr Walker, you've worked a miracle on that table. It's superb!'

'Thank you,' said Mr Walker. 'It's a fine piece. It deserved to be restored. Where was it you found it? In a cow shed?'

'Yes, can you believe it? The farmer used to keep his hay on it. It had been in his family for generations. He had no idea it was valuable.'

'And I'm sure you didn't tell him how valuable it was, either,' commented Mr Walker. He did not really like the way that some people who worked in antiques behaved. It wasn't really right. But he did like working on the furniture.

'It wasn't valuable in the condition it was in,' replied the shop owner. 'But it is now.'

'I could get £3,000 from a London shop for that,' she was thinking to herself.

'You must let me give you something,' she said to Mr Walker.

'You know that I won't accept payment,' replied Mr Walker. 'It's just my little hobby.'

'Well, let me give you something else,' said the woman, who did not feel it right that Mr Walker should work without some kind of payment. It would make it harder for her to ask him to do something again.

'Look,' she said. 'I found this bowl at a house sale last

week. It's oak and I think it's really old. It could be thirteenth century.'

Mr Walker picked up the bowl and immediately fell in love with it. It had been beautifully and simply made out of a piece of oak and it was certainly old. Mr Walker thought it could certainly be thirteenth or even twelfth century. It was hard to tell.

He could imagine it being used then. An elderly priest or a monk, even, in his monastery might have had it. He could imagine the monk in his simple room, near the church, keeping apples in it. It seemed to represent all he loved about wood and England, all in one simple bowl.

'Thank you,' he said. 'I'd like it very much.'

That night Mr Walker put the bowl on the table beside his bed so that it was the last thing he saw before he went to sleep.

That night he had a strange dream. He was in a monastery in England. He knew that it was England. Outside, through the window, he could see a park with an oak tree. There was a monk writing in a large book and beside him was his bowl. But it contained dried herbs, not apples. The strange thing was that the monk was talking and he couldn't understand what he was saying.

'It wasn't Latin,' Mr Walker told Greg Mount the following morning over coffee. 'I'd recognise Latin. But he was speaking some strange language.'

'Nothing strange about that,' replied Greg Mount. 'After the Norman invasion in 1066, lots of people didn't speak English. They spoke French. Richard I, despite what they show in the Robin Hood films, didn't speak a word of English. On the other hand, your monk could have come from Holland. This part of East Anglia always had closer relations with Holland than with London. Did you know that at one time more than a third of the population of Norwich was made up of foreigners? East Anglia would never have been such a rich region without all the foreign workers. After all, that's where your family probably came from.'

'What do you mean?' asked Mr Walker. 'Walker's a good English name.'

'Probably Flemish,' replied Greg Mount. 'They probably came to England from Holland in the sixteenth century, to find work.'

'What rubbish!' said Mr Walker, and went back to his class. 'I'm English,' he muttered to himself. 'Walker is an English name.'

The following week he took a book about local history out of the library. He found that Walker really was a Flemish name, as were Maynard and Kettle, other names he'd thought were English.

As he read he kept finding himself looking at the old oak bowl, and thinking about the French or Flemish monks who might have owned it. Slowly, Robert Walker began to admit to himself that he'd never actually thought about who the English were or where they had come from. He knew about the Saxons and the Romans and the Normans. But he'd always thought that after the Norman invasion, England had remained the same. The population hadn't changed. It had been English.

Now he realised just how wrong he had been. The country was always changing; people came and people left. Just like students at the school.

The following morning as he walked across the school grounds, he passed as usual under the branches of a large oak tree. It was thought to be about seven hundred years old. In the past Mr Walker had always thought of it growing up in a part of the world that had changed very little. Today he saw generations of foreigners walking under its branches.

He'd thought that he'd seen everything so clearly, but he'd been blind. England was a land that had always welcomed foreigners. It was a land made up of foreigners. Century after century, different people from different lands had come here, each generation in turn adding to the culture of England, bringing it new words and new customs. All of which were absorbed and became part of the nation he had always been so proud to think of as his.

'An oak tree becomes an oak bowl,' Mr Walker murmured to himself. 'All things change. Even me, perhaps. I really think that it's time I retired and spent more time restoring furniture. I could even start charging for it.'

Greg Mount watched Mr Walker as he walked towards his first woodwork class of the day. He couldn't think why, but it looked as if the old man was laughing.

One of the Lads

Luke Thomas was scared. He looked round at the boys sitting at the table and his mouth was dry. It was a Saturday, after the match, and he and 'the lads', as they called themselves, were waiting for a fight.

They were always waiting for a fight, waiting for a fight to happen.

'What do you think, Lukey?' asked Big Dave. He and the boys were in their usual pub and Luke had just bought them all another pint of beer.

'I don't know. Whatever you say,' replied Luke, who hadn't heard the question.

How often had he said those words, or words like them? Luke couldn't remember. He couldn't remember a time when the five of them had not been together. Sometimes in bed at night he thought that there must have been a time once when he had not been scared. A time before he met the lads.

It was his first week at school. He had met Dave and Mick first. Or they had spotted him. A new boy, a small boy, a target, a victim.

'Go on . . . give us your dinner money!' Dave had demanded. And after his head had been held down in the toilet, Luke had agreed. He would have agreed to give them anything they asked. The boys soon discovered that Luke would also do anything for them. They let him join the gang. He was one of them.

He was never an equal in the gang. He knew that. They knew that. But he was there because they needed him. He was useful. Soon the gang never went anywhere without Luke. When they decided to go to the park instead of going to school, Luke went with them. When they went out at night, so did Luke.

And they all went to football matches together. They were all Chelsea supporters. How could they be anything else? From the narrow Fulham streets where they grew up they could see the reflected lights from the stadium at Stamford Bridge where Chelsea played. Everyone at their school supported Chelsea. Their school had always been a Chelsea school. You could see it from the names cut into the doors.

Bonetti, Armstrong, Bentley – these were players that their fathers still talked about. More recent names were Zola, Vialli and Di Matteo. And cut deeply with the largest knives were other names: Eccles, Ginger Bill, King. These were the names of former fans, members of the Chelsea Headhunters, the names of the men who, during the seventies and eighties, had organised the violence among the Chelsea supporters.

When he was younger, Luke had gone to football matches with his dad, but after he joined the gang he went with the lads. They sat among all the other young Chelsea fans in the area that had always been called the Shed; where Chelsea supporters used to stand together and show how strong they were, where the Chelsea Headhunters were in charge, where the fans would cheer them just as much as they'd cheer the footballers.

Chelsea playing at home. Was there anything better?

Luke couldn't imagine it. He had grown up a fan, his dad had been a fan. All his memories were of matches. All of the fans jumping up like one person whenever Chelsea scored. All of them shouting together. It was the most exciting thing that Luke knew. And later, the only time that Luke ever stopped being scared was when he was at a match, because then he stopped being Luke. He was just part of the crowd, just another fan.

Before and after the matches was different. That was when the rival fans fought. There were always fights. That was how it was. Before the game, you met other Chelsea fans and you tried to attack the rival fans as they arrived at Stamford Bridge, or after the match, when they left the stadium. Or if you were lucky, you found small groups of rival fans in small streets where there were no police watching. Then you fought them.

The same thing happened in reverse whenever Chelsea played away from home. And everyone knew that Chelsea fans were the toughest, they were the dirtiest fighters. Everyone was afraid of them. Except perhaps for Millwall fans, who weren't afraid of anyone. But Millwall fans were animals, thought Luke. Everyone knew that.

The fact that there were seats now and you couldn't stand at games any more had changed things. These days there were lots of families at games – everyone eating and drinking together – and that had stopped most of the fighting at the games themselves. But there were always places where you could fight if you wanted to. And the lads and their friends wanted to fight. They wanted to become the new Chelsea Headhunters.

Football had become Luke's life way back, as early as he

could remember. He and the lads would spend the week first talking about the previous Saturday and then anticipating the next Saturday. He hardly ever bothered to go to school any more and he stopped doing any homework because the lads said that studying was a waste of time.

'Why?' asked his teachers.

'Why?' asked his parents. His parents didn't live together any more, but they would arrange to get together so that they could talk to him. The only time that they weren't shouting at each other, thought Luke, was when they were shouting at him.

'You used to enjoy school,' said his mother. 'Now your teachers say that you're never there. Why, Luke?'

'Because . . .' he answered. He never finished the sentence.

'Because I'm scared.' That was what he could have said. 'Because I like being needed. Because I don't know anything any more except the gang. Because I don't know anything any more except football.' He never said these things.

He copied the rest of the gang so completely that his teachers believed that he was the same as the others. They were all troublemakers. None of them was going to pass any exams.

Sometimes Luke forgot how he had joined the gang. He belonged to the gang, that was all that mattered. However, Luke never stopped being scared. He was always waiting for Dave or Mick or one of the others to realise that he wasn't really like the others. Waiting for them to throw him out of the gang. Or hit him. He wasn't actually sure which of these things he really feared most.

The gang had remained together even after they left school. There were four of them apart from Luke: Big Dave, Mick, Gerry and Steve. They left school without any qualifications, but Mick wanted to become an electrician and Gerry wanted to be a mechanic, so it had been decided that they would all go to the local technical college. Originally Big Dave had wanted to join the army, but he had failed the psychological test and so that option had been closed.

Luke had surprised the lads – and himself for that matter – by deciding that he wanted to be a carpenter. Big Dave agreed that it was OK. If the lads set up a building firm they would need a carpenter, so Luke was allowed to follow this individual route. And away from the lads, Luke was happy. He loved working with wood. He loved the smell of the pine as he sawed into it. He loved how the wood could be shaped under his hands. How he could make something that was useful and, at the same time, beautiful to feel and look at. He was good at his work. He was proud of his work. His new teachers were very pleased with him.

He never told the lads any of this. He never talked about his work to them. He always let them lead the conversations. It was safer that way.

'Luke, are you listening?' asked Mike. 'He hasn't heard a single word I've been saying,' Mike complained.

'He's thinking about that girl in the fish and chip shop,' laughed Steve. 'I've seen the way you look at her, Lukey!'

Luke thought that it was Steve who liked the blonde in

the fish and chip shop. But he just laughed and shook his head.

'Sorry,' he muttered. 'I was just thinking about the way they let that penalty shot go through on Wednesday.'

It was the perfect excuse. Always. The gang forgave anything if you used football as the excuse. You could bring any conversation back to a discussion of the game and how Chelsea had played.

'Yeah,' agreed Dave. He and the rest of the lads swore about the goalkeeper, who had allowed what should have been quite obviously an easy save to go into the back of his goal. Swearing was so much a part of the lads' way of speaking that none of them ever noticed it. Every remark, every description used words which had not only lost their shock value, but no longer had any meaning at all. Luke, however, had to remember not to use these words at home as they upset his mother, so he still remained aware of them. He thought that the others no longer heard them.

' "The Cat" would never have missed a save like that,' suggested Gerry. Neither he nor any of the lads had ever seen Bonetti, 'the Cat', but to all Chelsea supporters his name was sacred. They'd all grown up with stories of the famous goalkeeper. Their dads had seen him. Their dads still talked about him.

The lads all nodded. Luke looked at the clock behind the bar. It was six already and getting dark outside. It seemed that the chance of a fight had passed by now. The fans of the opposing team would either be in their coaches driving back home up the motorway or celebrating in the bars around Leicester Square and Soho, London's West

31

End. It looked as if the lads were happy just to spend the evening drinking. He began to relax.

'So,' said Dave firmly. 'As I was saying hours ago while Luke here was in another world, what about Amsterdam next month?'

The next England – Holland game was in Amsterdam. Dave had a friend who had a friend who lived in Amsterdam and could get some tickets.

'I'm up for it,' said Mike. 'I think we should go. Amsterdam in March. Cheap beer. England away. Three Lions against the Dutch. Yeah.'

Luke didn't know how he was going to find the money for the fare, but he was determined to go, too. If there was anything, any one thing that was almost as good as watching Chelsea at home, then it was watching England. Thousands and thousands of England fans waving their three lions scarves and the red cross of St George, thousands of men and boys painted red and white and shouting:

'England! England! England!'

'The time's right,' said Dave. 'We have to go to Amsterdam.' The lads nodded.

'This could be another Charleroi,' added Mike, remembering the stories of friends who had been in Belgium for Euro 2000. 'And this time we'll be there.'

'We'll give them a day to remember,' Steve laughed. 'Hey, Lukey,' he added, 'my glass is empty.'

'Luke got in the last round of drinks,' said Dave, who was feeling good at the thought of the promised fighting ahead. 'You get the round, Steve.'

Steve went to the bar and bought five more pints of beer.

'Why don't all those politicians understand that the fight is part of the game?' complained Dave as they drank.

Although Dave had never studied anything at school, his knowledge of football history was legendary. Luke knew that Chelsea had won the European Super Cup in '98, but he didn't know who had won it any other year. But Dave did. He also knew who had won the European Cup Winners' Cup, the League Cup, the Charity Shield and the FA Cup. Dave knew it all.

'How do you know that?' Luke often asked him.

'Just do, don't I?' Dave would say.

'Do you remember that Mr Forest back at school?' Dave asked the lads.

'The history teacher?' asked Luke.

'Yeah. Him,' said Dave. 'Well he lent me this book once. I think he wanted me to go to his lessons.'

The lads laughed. Dave had never gone to any history lessons.

'But the book was OK,' Dave told them. 'I've still got it. It's full of stuff.' Dave put his glass down firmly on the table that was damp with spilt beer.

The lads weren't quite sure what to say. No-one had ever seen Dave admit to reading before. Except for football magazines and books on how to repair cars. Steve thought it was a joke.

'You?' He laughed. 'Read a book? I don't believe it.'

Dave stood up and with one quick movement he picked up Steve's glass of beer and poured it over Steve's trousers. Then he sat down again.

'As I was saying,' said Dave, 'before I was interrupted. This book is full of all kinds of stuff. For example, did you know that when football began in the Middle Ages, it was a way for men to sort out their differences?'

'What do you mean?' asked Gerry cautiously. He drank his beer just in case Dave picked on him next.

'What do you think I mean? You're stupid, you know, you're really thick. You're so thick I don't know why Luke doesn't mistake you for a bit of wood.'

Gerry looked down at the floor. He was big, he was strong, and as a general rule he would fight anyone who insulted him. But Big Dave was different. He was their leader. None of the lads would ever hit Dave.

'Sort out their differences – fight,' continued Dave. 'Football started with men like us who just wanted a good fight. According to this book, it was always more a battle than a game.'

'Is that true?' asked Mike.

'Of course it's true. It's in a book, isn't it?' The lads nodded thoughtfully at this piece of information. After a moment Luke spoke.

'But didn't anyone try to stop it?'

'Good question, Lukey,' said Dave. Luke tried not to blush. Dave rarely said anything nice to anyone.

'Yeah, they did. Lots of them. Kings and politicians. They tried to ban football loads of times. But they never succeeded. And do you know why?'

The lads shook their heads.

'They never succeeded,' concluded Dave, 'because there have always been too many of us. We decide that there's going to be trouble and there's nothing anyone can do.'

'That's right,' agreed Mike. 'Amsterdam, here we come.'

'Here we come . . . here we come . . . here we come . . . '

sang the lads. Mike stood on the table, kicking the remaining glasses on to the floor, and the other drinkers in the pub decided it was time to leave. Luke went out with them so that he could ring Dave on his mobile phone at the first sight of a police car. It was Luke's job and he was always glad to do it. He felt that it gave him a moment of control over the lads. Though he always rang the second he saw the police cars make their way up the North End Road.

*   *   *

A few weeks later the lads were on a train to Amsterdam. They had sat up drinking all night on the boat from Felixstowe and were quiet on the train. Gerry had been sick on the station platform and Mike still looked rather green. Luke had been seasick on the boat, so hadn't drunk very much. He felt good now, but didn't let the others know this.

He looked out of the window at the passing countryside; there were canals everywhere. 'Just like a postcard,' he thought. It looked very neat and tidy. The train passed through fields and a small wood. Luke would have liked to stop the train there and get out and walk in the wood. He often dreamed of the woods. In his dream it was autumn, and red and yellow leaves were falling off the trees into his hands. But when he opened his hands, there was nothing there. He always woke up feeling strange after this dream.

Mike had bought large ham sandwiches and more beer for the journey, and Luke had to stop looking out of the window and concentrate on the lads' battle plans. They were in touch with some other fans and had arranged to meet in a bar. Dave had a map of where it was.

'It's five minutes from the station,' he told the others as they got off the train in Amsterdam. Luke was aware of the way that the locals looked at them. Dave as usual was wearing a dirty T-shirt that didn't quite reach the top of his jeans and Mike was drunk and shouting. Back home, Luke hadn't really noticed it, but here, against the neat rows of houses beside the canals, he thought that they looked awful. He began to wonder if he looked like that, too.

It was cold, but people in thick coats were sitting outside small cafés drinking coffee. Luke wanted to join them and watch the local people cycling over the small bridges across the canals. There was a heron on one of the boats beside a bridge. The bird flew off as they approached and Mike threw an empty beer can after it.

'Stop it, Mike,' said Luke.

'Did you say something?' asked Mike threateningly.

'Come on, you two,' said Dave. 'It's here.'

And there it was – an English pub in Amsterdam. Mike, Gerry, Steve and Dave shouted happily and ran towards it, but Luke hesitated.

'Lukey!' shouted Dave from the doorway. 'Get inside. It's your round.' Then, seeing a young Indonesian boy walk past, Dave picked up a glass from an outside table and threw it at him.

The boy ran down a side road. Dave cheered.

'One to us,' he shouted. 'One nil. One nil.' He went inside the bar, but Luke still hesitated outside. He was suddenly aware that he didn't want to be with the lads today. He didn't want to drink beer and fight. He wanted something else.

A young Dutchman had been passing on his bike when

Dave threw the glass. He'd stopped and now turned to Luke.

'What is wrong with you?' he asked. 'Why do you English behave like this? Why are you always so angry?'

Luke looked at him. He'd never thought about the gang like that. It was a question he'd never asked.

'Angry?' Luke asked the Dutchman. Then, before he could reply, said, 'I'm not angry.'

'But they are,' said the Dutchman. 'Your friends. They are angry. If you don't agree with them, you don't have to stay with them.'

It was an obvious statement. Someone could have said it to Luke years ago, but no one ever had. It was true, thought Luke. He didn't have to stay with the lads. He didn't even have to see them again.

Luke realised that ever since he had started his woodworking course he had begun to change. He just had not admitted it to himself. And he did have a choice. Only a few weeks ago his teacher had recommended him to a company producing handmade furniture in the country. The owner had visited the college and liked the way that Luke worked. And he'd offered him a job. Luke hadn't said yes, because he'd known that the lads wouldn't agree to it.

Now he realised that what the lads thought no longer mattered. They couldn't stop him. Not really. He could just go back home, ring the company, and pack up his things and go. He could make beautiful things with fine wood. He could walk in the woods and catch yellow and red leaves.

'They're not my friends,' Luke said to the departing Dutchman. 'Not any more,' he added to himself. He turned away from the pub and started to walk away. As he glanced back, he could see the four lads inside the bar. They were waving and shouting, but he couldn't hear them and the gestures they made meant no more to him than the actions of the chimpanzees he had once seen on a visit to London Zoo.

Frozen Pizza

'And this is your room . . .' Mrs Stonehouse opened the door.

The young man swallowed in amazement. There were dozens of painted rabbits all over the walls. There were white rabbits, black rabbits and brown rabbits. There were even rabbits painted on the bed itself and on the cushions on the bed.

'It was the children's room when they were small,' said Mrs Stonehouse. 'I hope you don't mind. But you said that you wanted a room with a desk and this is the only room we have with a desk in it. It's nice and clean, though. I dusted it only this morning.'

'No,' said the young man. 'I don't mind. It's fine. I expect that I'll soon get used to the rabbits.'

'I did them myself,' said Mrs Stonehouse, who always admired her own work. 'I painted them with a stencil.'

'I'm sorry,' said the young man. 'I don't know that word. With a what?'

'A stencil,' replied Mrs Stonehouse. 'You buy them at art shops.' She smiled. The young man could see that she was very proud of her work. 'It's like a thick piece of paper with shapes cut out and you stick it on the wall and paint inside the shapes. You can stencil all kinds of designs. Clever, isn't it?'

The young man thought it sounded like something he used to do at his nursery school. He had been about four years old at the time. He thought it was a rather strange thing for a grown-up woman to do, but he was too polite to say so.

'Well,' said Mrs Stonehouse, 'I expect that you'll want to unpack your things. I'll leave you in peace.'

The young man looked around the room and wondered whether he had made a mistake. Perhaps he should have stayed at the university and not chosen to have a room in the town. But he had thought that living in a family would help him to improve his English. It was already quite good. Good enough, in fact, for him to have won a place at the university to study science. He had a degree in his own country, but he wanted to carry out some additional research in England.

This was not what he had expected. He had expected a family of university people. People like his own family, who sat round the table talking and arguing at all times of the day and night. Although Mrs Stonehouse had said that she had two teenage children, the house was surprisingly tidy for a family with children. His own home, he realised, was always untidy. Every room was filled with books and piles of paper that threatened to fall down on to the floor whenever someone banged a door. This house was not at all like that. One of the first things he had noticed was that the entrance hall had been quite empty. There was just a small table with a telephone on it and a neat pad of paper with a pen beside it. Perhaps the kitchen would be more like his home, he thought.

The young man unpacked his clothes and put them away in the wardrobe. Then he piled his books on the desk, as there was no bookcase in the room. He was hungry. He looked at his watch. It was seven o'clock. He wondered what time the family had dinner. Mrs Stonehouse still seemed to be the only person in the house.

He walked downstairs and knocked on the door of the front room. He could hear sounds of laughter inside.

'Come in,' called Mrs Stonehouse.

The room was very pink and there were bows and little white baskets painted on the walls. He supposed that Mrs Stonehouse had done these too, with a stencil. He thought that the room looked horrible and imagined how his mother would laugh if she saw it.

Mrs Stonehouse was watching television. There was a quiz show of some kind. Two rows of contestants faced each other. They laughed whenever the man asking the questions said anything and they all clapped every time one of the contestants said anything. They reminded him of seals in the zoo. There were similar television shows in his country, but his family never watched them. They thought they were very stupid.

'Is there something you want?' asked Mrs Stonehouse, without looking up from the television.

'I'm sorry,' said the young man. 'I just wondered what time you had dinner.'

Mrs Stonehouse laughed. She had a strange laugh, like the bird-like sound of a mobile phone. 'We don't have dinner. We're all so busy; we just eat and run.'

The young man thought that was a strange thing to say when all she seemed to do was sit and watch television.

'Come with me,' she told the young man. 'I'll show you the kitchen.'

Mrs Stonehouse led him into the room at the end of the

hall. It was bright, very bright. The young man thought it might look better through sunglasses. The walls were yellow, the ceiling was yellow and the cupboards were yellow, bright yellow. It was like walking into the inside of a lemon. And there were, indeed, several lemons in the kitchen. And oranges and apples and bunches of grapes. All stencilled over the walls and the cupboards.

'It's . . . er . . . brilliant,' he said. He was trying to say that it was bright without saying how horrible he thought it was. But Mrs Stonehouse thought that he meant that it was very clever and she was pleased. She liked her work to be admired.

The young man looked round the room. Something was wrong.

'Excuse me,' he asked, 'where is the fridge?'

Mrs Stonehouse laughed again. 'It's here,' she said, opening a cupboard door. 'And the freezer is hidden here.'

The young man could not understand why anyone would want to hide a fridge or a freezer. He wondered where Mrs Stonehouse had hidden the cooker. What a strange kitchen this was, he thought. The only thing he recognised was the sink. It was a big old-fashioned white sink like his grandmother had at her farm. He wondered why Mrs Stonehouse did not have a nice new sink like his mother.

'It's a big sink,' he said.

'Yes,' Mrs Stonehouse replied. 'It's wonderful. I've been wanting a sink like this for years. It's a copy of an antique sink you know. They're very fashionable at the moment.'

'Oh,' said the young man. He felt more and more confused.

'And the cooker?' he asked. He couldn't see how you could hide a cooker in a cupboard, but in this house anything seemed possible.

'Oh, we don't have a cooker.' Mrs Stonehouse smiled. 'We'd never use it anyway. But here's the electric kettle and here's the sandwich-making machine, and this is the microwave.'

'I see,' said the young man. 'Do they live on sandwiches?' he wondered. 'But where do you cook?' He could see a shelf of big colourful cookery books on one wall.

'The poor boy,' thought Mrs Stonehouse. 'I suppose that in his country they don't have very much. I suppose that the women stay at home and cook simple food like they did here in England before I was born. I expect that he feels that he's very lucky to be able to stay in a house like this.'

'Oh, I don't cook.' She laughed. 'We're a very modern family. We don't waste our time on things like that and I've never been one for cookery. I love reading cookery books, of course,' she added. 'But that's different.'

The young man was now very confused. Mrs Stonehouse opened the freezer. 'Here,' she said. 'Everything you could want.'

The freezer was taller than the young man. Inside were boxes and boxes of frozen pizzas and ready-cooked meals. They filled all the shelves.

'You can help yourself to any of the packets. You just open the packet and put it into the microwave,' said Mrs Stonehouse. 'Nothing could be easier.'

The young man was still very puzzled. In his country he sometimes had pizzas with friends after going to the cinema. But they never had pizza at home, only in pizza restaurants. 'But when do you have dinner?' he asked.

'We don't have dinner,' she said. 'As I said, we all just help ourselves. I eat when I get back from my aerobics class and the kids grab something to eat when they get back from school before they go out. Though sometimes, like today, they go straight from school to their friends' houses. And Harry, that's my husband, he eats at different times. It depends whether he's working late or at the pub. We're a very independent family.'

'I was right,' she thought. 'In his country it must be very different. He's never been in a home like this.' She felt sorry for him.

'Her husband works late and goes by himself to the pub and her children go to their friends' houses. She must be very lonely,' thought the young man. 'That is why she doesn't cook proper meals.' He felt sorry for her.

Mrs Stonehouse was pointing out the contents of the square boxes that filled the freezer. 'There are frozen desserts, too,' she said. 'You don't have to defrost them; you can eat them straight out of the freezer. And we always have ice cream, too. At the moment we have chocolate, banana, and apple pie flavour.'

The young man suddenly remembered an article that they had discussed in his English class. It was from an English newspaper and explained how more and more people now ate ready-made meals, and how the contents of these meals were not what they appeared to be. So that if the packet said fish, you would not find an actual piece of fish inside, not like you would buy in a market, but bits of different fish squeezed together. This would then be covered with a strong-flavoured sauce so you wouldn't be able to taste the fish anyway.

The young man looked at the packets in the freezer and saw that on one packet of frozen fish dinner it actually said, 'contains real fish'. 'But what else could it contain?' thought the young man.

'What would you like tonight?' asked Mrs Stonehouse.

'Pizza will be fine,' said the young man.

'What kind of pizza?' asked Mrs Stonehouse.

There were so many kinds of pizza: pizza with mushrooms, pizza with ham and pineapple, and even baked bean pizza. 'Who could ever combine pizza with baked beans?' he thought. 'What a disgusting idea.'

'Cheese and tomato will be fine,' he said.

'Are you sure?' Mrs Stonehouse asked. 'He's obviously never had such a choice before,' she thought. 'It must be wonderful for him to come here.' 'What about mushrooms and olives with cheese and tomato?' she suggested.

'Yes, thank you,' he agreed.

'Fine,' said Mrs Stonehouse, taking a packet out of the freezer. 'Now, do you know how to use a microwave oven?'

The young man admitted that he had never worked a microwave before. So Mrs Stonehouse put the pizza inside the microwave and showed him how to set the timer.

'When it goes "ping" that means it's ready,' she said. 'So, now you're one of the family, all you have to do is come in and help yourself. You don't need to ask me.' She walked out of the door. 'Enjoy your pizza,' she said.

The young man found a knife and fork in a drawer. He put them on the table. Then he heard the microwave go 'ping'. He opened the door carefully, and using a cloth so that he didn't burn his hands, he took out the plate.

The pizza was awful. The base was soft and tasted of nothing and the sauce was too sweet. The olives and mushrooms had no flavour at all, but he ate it anyway because he was very hungry. 'How can people eat like this?' he thought. It was horrible to eat alone with nobody to talk to. The room was so bright, it was more like a hospital than a home. He felt quite miserable.

He washed up his plate and his knife and fork and went to his room. Later he heard doors open and someone went into the kitchen. He heard a 'ping'. Then, whoever it was climbed the stairs and another door opened and shut and he could hear loud music and the sound of a television.

'They all live by themselves,' he thought. 'How very strange. They don't talk to each other and they don't even meet up for dinner.'

He had never thought much about food before. At home, it was cooked by his mother, it was put on the table and he ate it. But now that he was away from home, he realised how much the food was part of home life. The smell of chicken soup filling the house as he walked in the door. His mother with flour up to her elbows, making a pie and talking and laughing at the same time. The feeling that the kitchen was the heart of the house and his mother was at the centre of the kitchen. Cooking, he saw now, was an essential part of family life back home.

The kitchen in this house was sad and lonely and no amount of yellow paint could change that.

The young man read a book until he was tired and then turned out his light. The rabbits danced around the walls.

The next morning the young man moved out. He went to a café and had some breakfast, and then went to the university housing office. The woman there listened to him and immediately found him another place to stay.

She also rang Mrs Stonehouse and told her that the young man had moved out.

'Was it the rabbits?' Mrs Stonehouse asked. 'I offered to put him in another room, but he said that he wanted a desk. He even had his own television. Really,' she continued, getting more and more angry. 'Compared with what he must have come from in his own country, you would have thought that he'd be grateful.'

'It's not that,' the woman at the housing office replied. She was writing on her list as she talked. Opposite Mrs Stonehouse's name she wrote, 'Unsuitable, except for independent teenagers. Note: no conversation practice, no home meal, frozen pizza.'

Sweetie

From: Nikki Apton <Nikkiapt@uk.com>
To: Robert Woodhouse <Robwoo@uk.com>
Date: Tuesday, April 3
Subject: Drinks

Hi Rob!

Thanks for your email. I do so agree with you, last night's talk was absolutely fascinating. If only all our seminars were like that! And I was really glad you came up and spoke to me. It's so great to find someone who can share the same enthusiasms. I wish I'd taken notes!

Yeah, I'd love to meet up again for a drink sometime. I don't think the college bar, though. It's so packed with first-years (ugggh!). How about that new wine bar in Market Street? I've heard it's OK. But whatever you think . . .

See you soon . . .

Nikki

From: Nikki Apton <Nikkiapt@uk.com>
To: Sue Fordham <Sueford@uk.com>
Date: Tuesday, April 3
Subject: New man

Susie! Hi!

How's the work going? I can see you writing away there with a pile of books all round you. Anyone would think that one goes to the library to work!! Seriously though, if you've got any ideas on what Mr Shakespeare was thinking of by bringing on a gatekeeper to go on and on just when he's got to the interesting bit of the play (just where someone got killed), then do throw a few ideas my way. Or let me have a quick read of your notes. You're so clever.

Anyhow, sweetie, to the point, to the point as Mr Shakespeare might have written, but never did. I've met this amazing guy.

It was at that talk last night. I only went along because Mrs Martins was so rude this week about my work that I wanted to be able to say that I even went to literature talks that weren't compulsory. I'm surprised you weren't there, but I expect you were writing your essay. You'd have loved it. It was all about Shakespeare's women, you know the kind of thing, how they were all played by boys and how you had boys playing women dressed as boys . . . etc, etc.

So there I was, being bored out of my mind. In fact I was only half listening. I was wondering if purple nails were really too last year and thinking what colour I should paint them next. But then I noticed the guy in front of me.

Well, I only noticed him when he turned round. I suppose I was yawning rather loudly. When he turned round I thought he was going to agree with me how boring it all was. I was about to whisper that I'd heard better arguments around my parents' dinner table, and that was saying something!! But then I realised that he wanted me to be quiet. He was enjoying the talk!! Normally I'd have just ignored anyone who tried to make me keep quiet, but then I looked at him properly and he was amazing. I mean not your usual student good-looking, but film star good-looking – sort of Hugh Grant hair and Mel Gibson blue eyes. I tell you he was so much the 'real thing' I almost blushed. But I didn't. Promise.

So I managed to convince him that my yawn was a cough and muttered, 'Sorry.' Then I smiled at him and he smiled at me.

After the talk ended, he came up to me. He's called Robert and he's doing a postgraduate degree in creative writing – yes, really, one of them!! The creative writing stars! And, can you believe it, he's not only written a novel, but there's a publisher interested in it! Even my mother would be impressed.

And he's emailed me already today and asked me if I fancy a drink. If? *When* would be a better question. I thought about playing it cool but thought that he looked so cool himself there wasn't any point. After all, when you look like that *and* you're brilliant, no girl is ever going to say no, is she? So I said yes. So watch this space.

Oh, I must go and iron some clothes in case he asks me out tonight.

Sweetie, I just haven't got time now to look up all those

boring books. Please, please, can I look at your notes? Thank you so, so much, you're such a good friend.

Kiss, kiss . . . and keep up the good work. Well, one of us has to!

Your excited friend

Nikki

From: Nikki Apton <Nikkiapt@uk.com>
To: Sue Fordham <Sueford@uk.com>
Date: Wednesday, April 4
Subject: What to wear . . . help!!

Susie

You star! Thank you so much for your notes. So many references!! I don't know how you find the time to look up all those books. I just haven't had a moment. I mean it's not as if we can spend all our time writing essays. We have to go to all these lectures and seminars, too. Mind you I missed this morning's seminar. Did Mrs Martins notice? I spent so much time last night trying to decide how I should look when I see Robert next that I didn't get to bed till after 2 am. So I slept till lunchtime. As a result I've felt exhausted all day. But I am trying to work. Really!

I think what I need is a new pair of black jeans. I could wear them with that little white top that stops just above my waist. I think that would be perfect. It would look good without looking as if I'm trying too hard. It's all so difficult, isn't it? At least all this worry has stopped me eating. You're so lucky not worrying about what you look like. When you've got a reputation like I have for having a certain kind of style, it's a real responsibility.

The bad news is the bank won't give me any more money. I put my card into the machine this morning and it came straight back out. So I'll have to borrow some more from my dad. I expect I'll think of an excuse. And he's so pathetically proud of my having got a place at university.

Just because he had to go to work straight from school. He has no idea what it's like here. He thinks it's like school but harder.

See you later . . . what are you doing for supper tonight?
Nikki

Daddy, sweetie

What can I say? It's too awful to have to ask you again, but you did say that you'd help with books. I never realised that I'd need so many.

I know you said that things were getting difficult at work and you needed to be careful in case you were made redundant. Isn't that a horrible word?! No one ever says they're firing people any more. They just make them redundant. But it's just as horrible. Anyhow, I'm sure you're worrying about nothing. They wouldn't dare get rid of you. You're so clever, and you've been there for years and years. They could never do without you.

I'm sorry to have to get back to money, but I do need it urgently. The books I need are never in the library. I think everyone must go in at midnight, like ghosts, to get them before I get there. So if I'm not going to get the most awful marks for my next essays, I just have to buy them.

There's a second-hand bookshop here at the university, so it's not quite as expensive as buying new books. Actually they are real bargains and I can sell them again after I've written my essays, so I *will* try and pay you back. I promise.

If you could send me another £50, I'd be so relieved, and then I can finish this essay and make you proud of me.

Give mummy my love. She sounded cross with me when I rang home yesterday. I don't know why she doesn't get herself an email address, and then I could write to her. She was very sarcastic when I said that and said, 'The Royal Mail hasn't gone out of business as far as I know. I think you'll find, Nicola, that stamps are still on sale in most parts of Great Britain. And envelopes.' Ha! Ha! It's just that letters are so slow. So last century.

Thank you so much Daddy. You're such a sweetie. And don't worry about the job. It'll be fine.

Lots and lots of love

Your hard-working daughter

Nikki

From: Nikki Apton <Nikkiapt@uk.com>
To: Sue Fordham <Sueford@uk.com>
Date: Saturday, April 7
Subject: Date update

Hi Susie!

I've managed to drag myself to the library, but there's no way that I'm going to be able to do any work today. I'm exhausted. Rob and I talked for hours. I think the new jeans were just right. Daddy came up with the money. He's such a sweetie, he believes everything I tell him.

Rob is really impressive, but I have to confess he is a bit intense. I know he's an intellectual, but he does go on about politics and things. Last night we were happily drinking cocktails – yes, I've actually met someone who can afford my taste in drinks!! So there we were drinking peach juice and champagne, and I was wondering how soon he was going to kiss me, when he starts talking about refugees in Britain. I mean, who cares? Why do these people want to live here anyway? But, according to Rob, the government doesn't have a consistent policy, and lots of refugees are living for months in old army camps. Well at least they're safe and their lives are probably better than they were in their own countries. But Rob went on and on about how there is no proper education for refugee children and that something ought to be done about it. I can't think why he thought I'd be interested. Like the song says, girls just want to have fun. And politics isn't fun. Right?

Anyhow, it was our first date and I didn't want an argument. I hate arguments, they give me a headache. So I made interested noises and agreed with him. And that was fine. Men are so pathetic. All you have to do is say, 'I agree,' every few minutes and they think you're brilliant.

But it turns out that he isn't only interested in all that politics stuff. He likes movies, too. So tonight we're going to the cinema to what Robert calls 'a popcorn movie'. This is his definition of an American film with lots of action and chases and things being blown up. Are there any other kinds of film?

I have a feeling Rob also likes foreign movies, the kind you only find in small specialist cinemas. I hate those films. You have to work really hard reading the subtitles in English and no one ever does anything. They all talk too much. So boring. Oh, sorry, I forgot. You like those kinds of films, don't you?

And yes, before you ask, we did kiss, but only a friendly goodnight kiss at my door. He smells of lemons, did I tell you? Delicious! I can't wait for tonight!

In fact I think I'm going to spend the rest of the day getting ready. Then I'll have a long bath and throw in lots of that new perfume I bought last week. I just haven't got the energy to open a book. So can you help me again, sweetie? Tell me what I'm supposed to do before Monday's seminar. Thank you so much . . . you're wonderful.

Your tired friend
Nikki

From: Nikki Apton <Nikkiapt@uk.com>
To: Robert Woodhouse <Robwoo@uk.com>
Date: Saturday, April 7
Subject: Hi

Just a terribly quick note. I saw you downstairs in the library as I came up, but I didn't want to disturb you. In any case, I've got so much work to do before Monday's seminar that if you came up here you wouldn't be able to see me because I'm surrounded by so many books! But I just wanted to say how much I enjoyed last night. It was so refreshing to talk to someone who really thinks about things. So many friends – my friend Sue, for example – just don't care about the important things in life.

But tonight we'll have a bit of fun. Why not? We deserve it.

See you later . . .

Love

Nikki

From: Nikki Apton <Nikkiapt@uk.com>
To: Sue Fordham <Sueford@uk.com>
Date: Monday, April 16
Subject: Careers – who needs them!

Susie, my love . . .

Thank you so much for covering up for me at the seminar today. But I don't know why you say it's the very last time. I mean nobody really needs to go to seminars. It's not as if they count towards your degree. Or only a bit. You can still get a degree if you pass the exams, can't you?

Anyhow, I wasn't at the dentist's. I was asleep. Rob was even more exhausting than ever last night. He insisted on showing me all these leaflets about all these people who are in jails all over the world because they disagree with their governments. Or something. As if I cared. Not that I let him know. But he did begin to sense that my concentration was wandering because I kept playing with my hair. Then, at last, there was a film on the TV that he liked, so we could watch that instead. Actually I thought it was rather boring, too, but he said it was a very important early western. I can't remember the name of the director. You probably know it.

Then this afternoon was the end. It was too awful. I had an appointment with the careers office, but I don't know why I bothered. It was useless. They didn't have any jobs that sounded in the least bit exciting. They kept talking about career paths and 'getting the right kind of work experience'. I just wanted to say like that character – you

59

know the one I mean in that Tom Cruise movie – 'Show me the money!' Who needs career paths? I just want to get to London as quickly as possible and earn as much money as I can. For a start, I have to pay off my student loan. I don't see why my parents couldn't have given me more money themselves. Only a few years ago university education was free and you got grants. My parents' generation were so lucky, and there was my father not even taking advantage of it. Just because his dad made him go to work at sixteen.

There were lots of leaflets in the careers office from companies who hire graduates and train them for 'senior management', whatever that means. Can you see me as a manager in a shop or a factory? It was such a waste of time. I had to fill in forms and do some kind of psychological test. It was all so stupid. I hate those things.

'How do you see yourself in five years' time?' the woman asked me. She had one of those awful old-fashioned dresses, like shirts, that button all the way down. And she had one of those nasty small faces, like a rat. 'Well, I don't see myself in a pathetic job like yours,' I nearly told her. But of course I didn't actually say it.

What I did say was: 'In five years' time I can see myself being rich and successful and wearing designer labels and drinking in London wine bars.' I smiled at her. I *was* trying. 'I was thinking maybe that I could work in the City,' I added.

I read in a magazine about bank employees getting a million pounds on top of their salaries. The City of London sounded like my kind of place – champagne bars, sports cars, lots of money!

'I don't see either mathematics or economics among your qualifications,' the careers woman replied. 'What kind of job are you thinking of doing in the City? Secretary? Waitressing?'

Can you believe it? How rude! I mean in two years I'll be a university graduate and she asked me if I'd thought of being a waitress! I was furious. I ought to report her to someone. She had no right to speak to me like that. It's jealousy. I always get it from unattractive women. They just can't bear to think that a girl who looks like me can have brains, too.

So, sweetie, I'm really fed up. Come over and have a drink later and cheer me up while I get ready to go out with Rob. You can help me choose what to wear.

Your depressed friend

Nikki

From: Nikki Apton <Nikkiapt@uk.com>
To: Elizabeth Martins <Elizamart@uk.com>
Date: Tuesday, April 17
Subject: Seminars

Dear Mrs Martins

I was really upset when I got your letter. I mean I can't
be the only one who sometimes misses your seminars. They
are awfully early and it's not as if I'm not writing my essays.
It's probably because I stay up so late working that I
sometimes oversleep. And I don't think that your
comments about me putting pressure on my friend Sue
Fordham are in the least bit true.

And I do read the books on my reading list. I can't think
why you should say that I don't seem to have ever opened a
book.

This degree course means a lot to me and I am doing my
best. I can't believe that what I say at seminars could make
such a difference to my getting a degree or not. I'm just not
at my best working in a group.

But I really will try harder to be punctual and not to
oversleep. So please give me another chance.

Yours

Nikki Apton

From: Nikki Apton <Nikkiapt@uk.com>
To: Sue Fordham <Sueford@uk.com>
Date: Tuesday, April 17
Subject: That cow Mrs Martins!

I'm so upset, you just don't know! I thought you were my friend. What did you say to Martins? She says that I forced you into covering for me. You know that's not true. I've never forced you to do anything. How dare she say that!

And now I've got to go to her awful seminars or she's going to put a fail against my name, and she says because I don't get good marks for my essays either, if I fail my seminars, I'll fail the year and won't be allowed to finish my degree.

It's just not fair. I do as much as I can. I really do think you could be more helpful.

I'm so depressed by it all that I think I'll have to go shopping and buy myself some new clothes. The trouble is I don't have any money and the last time I asked my dad for some more, I got a horrible letter from my mother telling me that I was selfish and that things were difficult. She's always looking for ways to be nasty to me. Just because daddy likes buying me things.

I saw you talking to Robert earlier. What was he saying about me? Something nice I hope. He was a bit strange yesterday. Just because I thought that Lévi-Strauss made designer jeans. How could I know he was some kind of famous writer? I'm beginning to think that Rob's not worth all the effort. Perhaps I need someone who isn't so serious all the time. If only he wasn't so attractive. But he is and I know that most of the females on the creative writing course are crazy about him. It's lucky that he happens to like me, isn't it?

I feel that everyone is against me today, so please come over later and cheer me up. It probably wasn't your fault about Martins. She just hates me anyway because of the way I look.

See you later
Nikki

From: Nikki Apton <Nikkiapt@uk.com>
To: Robert Woodhouse <Robwoo@uk.com>
Date: Tuesday, April 17
Subject: Disaster

Rob

I've just had the most awful letter from one of my lecturers, Elizabeth Martins. Do you know her? She teaches us nineteenth century Romantic Poetry – new ways of looking at Keats and Shelley, all that kind of thing. And she tells me that she's going to fail me because I've missed a couple of seminars. It's so, so unfair!

Now I've got to think of something really clever to say before this Thursday about Wordsworth and the French Revolution, so can you help me? You're so clever and I know you know everything about those poets.

Will you come round later? I'll be so, so grateful. I know you've got a huge essay to write yourself, though it's too long and important to be called an essay isn't it? You've got your dissertation to write. But this is an *emergency*! I'm relying on you to be there.

Thank you my sweet
Your Nikki

From: Nikki Apton <Nikkiapt@uk.com>
To: Sue Fordham <Sueford@uk.com>
Date: Wednesday, April 18
Subject: Last night

Susie . . .

What *is* the matter? Just because I forgot that both you
and Rob were coming over and just because I met some
people and went out for a few drinks, I really don't think
that you had to speak to me like that. I know that you and
Rob had work to do and were only there because I asked
you. But you didn't have to come over if you didn't want
to.

If you hadn't been so horrible, I would have thanked you
for talking to Rob. I know that the two of you both like
lots of the same things. So it was nice for him to have a bit
of a conversation while he was waiting for me. And you
should be grateful, too, because you would never have got
the chance to talk to him if he wasn't my boyfriend, would
you? I mean *I* know how interesting you are – you're my
friend. But boys only notice what a girl looks like.

Anyhow I need to talk to you today because I've had a
terrible letter from my father. He says that his firm has
gone through lots of changes and they're getting rid of all
the experienced people. They just want young people, he
says. So he's been made redundant. It's too awful. It could
be ages before he gets another job and I can't ask him for
any more money right now and I really want that little red
dress I saw in town yesterday.

It's all too terrible.
Your desperate friend
Nikki

Oh Rob

I'm so, so sorry about last night. Please don't be angry. It was because I was so upset about everything that I stopped for a moment to have a quick drink.

What I haven't told you – because I didn't want you to worry about me – is that there are lots of problems at home. My father has been made redundant and it's been a terrible worry for us all. I just can't think about anything else. So that's why I stopped for a drink.

Anyhow, thank you so much for being such a sweetie and talking to Susie. It was really kind of you to talk to her for so long. She's so serious! I keep telling her to lighten up, but she doesn't listen to me. And her clothes! That old sweater she was wearing last night. Where do people get clothes like that? Poor sweetie. I do try to give her some advice now and again on make-up and I've even offered her some of my old clothes, but of course they are all much, much too small for her. She really ought to make more of an effort and lose some weight, but I don't think she really understands how important it is to look good.

I've still got that seminar coming up, but I don't think I can face it. I'll have to try and talk to Mrs Martins. Isn't life difficult? I just don't know what to do.

Please don't be angry just when I need you. Come and talk to me later. Please??

Your very sorry

Nikki

From: Nikki Apton <Nikkiapt@uk.com>
To: Peter Apton <Peterapt@globlink.uk.com>
Date: Wednesday, April 18
Subject: Everything's too awful

Darling Daddy

Yes, of course I sympathise with you about your work and all that. But I'm sure that you'll get another job soon. Just saying that middle-aged men of forty-eight aren't given jobs these days isn't going to help you. You have to be positive!! Like you always tell me.

Everything is just awful here, too. There's a woman called Elizabeth Martins who hates me and wants me to fail. She says that she's going to get me thrown out. So you can see that you're not the only one with problems.

But I try to be positive and just keep on going. And you must do the same.

I can't believe that you're serious about cutting my allowance. How can I live? I thought you wanted me to be at university. But now I think that you don't really care.

I don't think anyone cares about me.

Your desperate daughter

Nikki

Mummy darling

I'm so glad that you're finally using daddy's computer. That means I can write to you more often because it's so much easier than letters and, unlike phones, I can write to you in the library without interrupting my work.

I've just had the most awful email from daddy. He says that you and he have been talking and you can't afford to continue giving me my allowance. And why don't I take out a student loan? Now, I didn't want to worry daddy, he's got so much to worry about, but I've already taken out a student loan and I've spent it. So I can't exist for the rest of this year without my allowance. I'd just starve.

Mummy, you must know what it's like. I have to have a few clothes, and everything's so expensive. And these days girls are expected to pay for their own drinks. I do *try* to be careful with money, but it's so hard.

So Mummy, sweetie, could you please, please have a word with daddy, so that I can stay here next term. Otherwise I'll just have to give it all up and become a waitress or work in a supermarket or something. It's just too awful to think about. I know that daddy listens to you.

Lots of love
Nikki

From: Nikki Apton <Nikkiapt@uk.com>
To: Elizabeth Martins <Elizamart@uk.com>
Date: Thursday, April 19
Subject: Your letter

Dear Mrs Martins

I've just received your official letter and I can't believe that you've decided to fail me. It's not my fault if I'm just too upset about my family to do any work. Please can't you give me another chance? I really do want to get my degree. Please can I come and talk to you?

Yours
Nikki Apton

From: Nikki Apton <Nikkiapt@uk.com>
To: Peter Apton <Peterapt@globlink.uk.com>
Date: Friday, April 20
Subject: How could you!

Daddy

I'm so upset I can hardly write this. I just can't believe you meant all those horrible things you just said to me on the phone. You say that you can suddenly see me as I really am. And that mummy was right all along, but you didn't want to admit it. It's just not true. Mummy has always wanted to see the worst in me. I don't know why.

I just don't know why you had to phone Mrs Martins. OK, so I was exaggerating a bit in my last letter. But Mrs Martins has never liked me. I don't know what she said to you, but it seems you find it easy to believe her and not me.

And then you said you'd tried to ring me lots of times, but I was always out. It's not fair. I was only out twice and I was mostly working in the library. That's what I'm here for. Nobody seems to understand just how hard I've tried. But why did you have to talk about me to Sue? You said Sue told you that I hadn't told you the truth and she thought you ought to know the truth. She's just jealous of me. And there's something else. She's jealous of my boyfriend. So that's why she's horrible about me. It's not true that I spend a fortune on clothes. I have bought a few clothes, but I needed them!

And yes, it's true that I have taken out a student loan in

addition to my allowance, but I needed the money. You've just *no* idea how expensive it is these days to exist at university.

And I only missed a few seminars. Anyone can oversleep. They shouldn't start at such a ridiculously early hour. It's not my fault.

Anyhow, your ringing Mrs Martins has just made everything worse. Now she won't listen to me, and the university will fail me and I won't be able to stay here after this term. So that's what you've done with your telephone calls. You've ruined my life and I hate you.

I suppose I will have to get some dreadful job now and that will be the end of my life.

So I hope you're happy.

Your very unhappy daughter

Nicola

From: Nikki Apton <Nikkiapt@uk.com>
To: Sue Fordham <Sueford@uk.com>
Date: Saturday, April 26
Subject: Goodbye
cc: Robert Woodhouse <Robwoo@uk.com>

This is my last email because after today the university says that the number they gave me to use the computers won't work any more. I thought that nothing could get any worse, but it has. Not that anyone cares how I feel.

Daddy is in hospital because of his heart and mummy says it's my fault because I made him so upset. It wasn't me who fired him from his job. I think she's too horrible. She says he's going to be OK, but he won't be able to work again. So I have to get a job now and keep myself.

Not that either of you care. I thought you were my friends, but all the time you were making plans behind my back. Well, sweeties, you may think you're both very clever, but I think that showing each other some of my old emails is a terrible thing to do. I'd never do anything like that.

I hope that you both bore yourselves stupid with your clever books and foreign films. You're both just right for each other. I don't need friends like you anyway. Soon I'll have a good job and be earning lots of money while you two will still be poor students. You don't need a degree to be successful, anyway. I should have realised that ages ago.

So, goodbye.
Nikki

The Star Reporter

Have you ever had that one moment when you know that if you do something, it will change the rest of your life? I don't mean saying 'yes' when somebody asks you to marry them, but maybe I do mean that as well. Have you ever had one of those moments when you know that what you are going to do next will change the rest of your life? Have you ever been in that position? If you have, then you will understand what happened to me.

I had a friend, well not really a friend, just a girl I used to talk to in the students' union bar, and she was on holiday once in southern Spain. She was about eighteen at the time, working in Spain during her gap year after school and before coming up to university. She was on a bus in Granada, waiting for it to leave, and this guy tapped on her window. She said that he was the most beautiful man she'd ever seen, a traveller, one of a band of musicians – she could see their van. And he gestured for her to get out of the bus and go with him. And she wanted to, but she didn't. And she said that she'd never forget that moment and I know that she's right. She won't. You see you don't get that many moments in a life.

I know. Because my life has changed. Completely. And this is how it happened.

The day had started well. It was Tuesday morning and I was in the *Student News* office for an early meeting. I'm sure you've heard of *Student News*. It's been the winner of the University Newspaper of the Year award for ten years in a row; three former editors have top jobs on major newspapers. It's the newspaper every Media Studies student wants to write for. That's why many of them choose this university. And I was the award-winning news editor – voted the student most likely to succeed after uncovering a big property fraud in the city last year. I was the star reporter.

So there I was with the rest of the team in the tiny cupboard we called the office: two big filing cabinets, a table with a couple of computers, and some chairs that looked as if they had lost their cushions halfway through the last century; walls covered with grey paint with bits missing where people had stuck things up, a view through the window of concrete and dustbins – you know the kind of place. But none of that mattered to us. We weren't there to admire the view, but to show how clever we were.

I'd already had a few articles in the *Independent* and the *Sunday Times*, and everyone knew that I'd been promised a job as soon as I finished my degree later that year. This had made the editor really furious.

Angela. That was our editor's name, a real reporter, a bit like those tough American reporters I used to watch in old movies. I'd never liked her much, but I did respect her. She was a good editor. She had a nose for a story, as we say. She could always smell a good story. She had a feeling for things that excited people. You could see that she would become a good journalist. And that is what she wanted after university. She was desperate to get a job in one of the tabloids.

Let me explain. There are two kinds of newspapers:

First, there are the serious newspapers, the broadsheets, the big newspapers that you can't open in a bus without hitting the person sitting next to you. You're talking about the *Guardian*, the *Independent*, the *Telegraph*, *The Times* and their Sunday editions. Some people call them 'the heavies', and not just the poor delivery boys and girls who can only bike around with half a dozen copies because they weigh so much. No, it's because they are said to be intellectually heavyweight. And compared to the other kind of newspaper, they are.

Second, there are the tabloids. These are small papers which have huge headlines, sometimes only one word that almost fills the page. This is great because they are not intended for people who actually want to read. They contain stories about soap stars and other famous people, and about the events in soap operas and the weekly issue. This is what they think is news. They take a story and decide what the issue is and then demand that the government do something about it immediately. It is quite possible that they demanded the opposite a few months ago, but they assume that their readers don't remember such things, and they are usually right. When it rains, the tabloids scream, 'Stop this flooding!' and when it doesn't rain they scream, 'Where's the water?' They love crime because then they can have full-page headlines that shout, 'WANTED!' or show some face and scream, 'Is this the face of the most evil man in Britain?'

I've always hated the tabloids and the way they react to the news. They are like two-year-olds who scream when they are hungry or lose a toy. I've never thought that their attitude to world affairs was grown-up. Today I feel differently. I think that what they do in order to increase their readership is actually evil. But then I would say that, wouldn't I, after what happened?

Angela had always wanted to work for a tabloid newspaper. But because *Student News* won awards funded by a broadsheet, the tabloids weren't interested in her. Not then, anyway.

So, it was another Tuesday morning, another ordinary editorial meeting. Or so I thought. I was only half listening to Angela, who was dominating the meeting as usual.

'Is everyone here?' she asked. 'I don't know about any of you, but I want to get back home soon; I've got a lot of work to do.'

'She just wants to get home to watch the soaps on television,' my friend Laura, the features editor, whispered to me. I laughed and Angela frowned at me.

'I hope you've come here with a few good ideas for next week's top story, Mike.'

I hadn't really thought much about next week's issue. I had been working on an essay until late the previous night. I still had to get my degree. However, I wasn't going to let Angela know that.

'Yes.' I smiled at Angela. 'I've got a great idea,' I said.

And I had. It had just come to me right then.

'Good,' said Angela. 'Can you share it with us?'

'Sure,' I said. 'You know how the university sold off some land near the river for building last year? For building a new housing estate? Well, think about all the floods we've been having. There's a real danger with land that close to a river. Actually, I wouldn't be surprised if the area used to be a flood plain – you know, where fields beside rivers were kept empty because they flooded every year, and that stopped the river flooding the town.'

Angela nodded. I knew she was interested.

'A few families have moved into the new estate,' I continued, 'and I think the river may have flooded already. And I bet no one told them that their new houses were likely to flood. I bet no one told them that the houses were on an old flood plain.'

'I like it,' said Angela immediately. 'Mike, you go and interview the families and take Sue with you to do the photos. John, you look on the Internet and see if you can find some old maps that show the area. If you can't find what you need online, then go to the library in town. They have a local history section. Sue, I want you to find some good pictures of other estates built on flood plains that have flooded recently. We'll make it a two-page news special.'

That's what Angela is like. I told you she was a good editor. She knows what makes a good story and she knows how to make sure that every detail of the story is properly shown.

And so that was how it started.

I went down to the new estate with Sue, our photographer. There were only about six finished houses and five families had moved in. The river had come up as far as the front doors and there was thick mud everywhere. It was awful. And it smelt. Goodness knows what was in the river, but it certainly wasn't clean water.

As we arrived, a young mother was trying to lift a buggy with a baby inside over the mud. She'd been to the supermarket and was carrying several bags of shopping.

'Here!' I said. 'Let me help you!'

'Wait,' said Sue. 'That's a perfect shot!'

She took a picture, but as she did so, the mother, who wasn't much older than me, heard the sound.

'No!' she shouted, and put her hands over her face. She dropped the buggy and if I hadn't jumped forward, I think the baby would have fallen sideways into the thick mud. I lifted the buggy out of the mud and put it inside the doorway of her house.

'It's OK,' I said gently. 'We didn't mean to upset you. We're from the university. We're doing a story about the flood for the student newspaper.'

'You're students?' asked the mother. She seemed relieved. She looked around at the sea of black mud. 'And you just want to write about this?'

'Yes,' I said. But wheels were turning in my reporter's head. 'What other story is there?' I was wondering.

'If you don't want to be photographed, it's not a problem,' I said. Sue gave me a dirty look. 'It was just that the baby in his buggy made a great picture. It really shows people what you have to put up with here.'

'It's been terrible,' the mother murmured. 'Ever since it started to rain last month. I thought the water was going to come right inside the house. But it didn't.' She smiled. She looked much younger when she smiled.

'Do come in,' she said. 'My name's Carol. And this . . .' she stroked her baby's cheek . . . 'this is Robbie.'

'Why don't I talk to Carol while you see if some of the other families will be willing to let you photograph them?' I suggested to Sue.

'OK,' agreed Sue, though I knew that she still wanted to

take more shots of Carol trying to lift her baby over the mud.

'Some of the other families may have small children, too,' I added.

Sue went off and I helped Carol take her shopping indoors. The house was almost empty. You could see that Carol didn't have much money, but everything was spotlessly clean. She clearly spent all her money on her baby, and apart from baby food, one of the things in her bag was a new toy for Robbie. It was a round container with different shaped holes – you know – round, square, triangular. And a bag full of round, square and triangular blocks. Robbie loved it. You could see that. He took each block and tried to get it through each hole in turn.

'It was a bit expensive,' Carol confessed, 'but I thought he'd enjoy it. And it would help him learn things.' It was clear just how much her baby meant to her.

I liked Carol. Let's get that straight. And I could see that she was a marvellous mother. So I could have just asked her a few questions about the flooding and walked away. But I didn't. There had been something about the way she'd reacted to Sue that bothered me.

She didn't want any pictures. And she didn't like journalists. Something had happened to her in the past; I was sure of it. I decided to find out who she was.

It wasn't difficult. The building company had a record of all the people who had rented the houses and Angela had already emailed it to me. Number 4, the house we had visited, had been rented by Carol Peterson.

The name Carol Peterson didn't mean anything to me and I couldn't find anything on the Internet. But then

I typed Carol Peters and hit the search button too soon. It was just a mistake. But it told me who Carol really was. She was Carol Peters. There was loads of stuff about her.

At the time of the trial, I was only ten years old, but I do remember people talking about it. I suppose that everyone was talking about it. Carol was eleven years old then. It was revealed during the trial that she'd had a terrible childhood herself: her parents drank and were violent. She'd been a lonely child, never made any friends. But she loved looking after children. And even though she was so young, lots of mothers let her look after their babies. I think that's why they were so angry. They all felt that it could have been their baby who died.

No one ever found out exactly what had happened. Carol said that she'd put the baby on a slide and he'd fallen off and smashed his head. But the blood was on the other side of the park, near a wall. So the police thought that she'd hit the baby to stop it crying. She said that she'd taken the baby over there after the accident. She'd wanted to hide away.

The jury didn't believe her. They decided that she'd murdered the baby. She was sent to a prison for young people and stayed there until she was sixteen. After that, no one knew what had happened to her.

I was reading one final report when Angela came into the office. The article had been written by a tabloid reporter who had waited for her to leave the prison, but missed her and then wrote that Carol was a monster who should stay in prison for the rest of her life. Angela read the article over my shoulder before I noticed she was there. It took her about two seconds to make the connection between Carol Peters and Carol Peterson.

'How long have you known about this?' she asked me.

'I've only just discovered it,' I told her.

'And were you going to tell me?' she enquired.

'Of course,' I lied.

I knew what was going to happen next: Angela would ring up one of her new contacts at one of the tabloid newspapers. And that is exactly what she did. The tabloid press had a great time.

'WE FIND CHILD KILLER'S SECRET HOME!' they screamed.

'IS THIS CHILD SAFE?' they asked about Robbie. The law in Britain protects children, so they weren't allowed to mention his name or take pictures of him. They took pictures of a teddy bear in the garden instead. It wasn't even Robbie's teddy bear; one of the tabloid reporters had put it there. Near the front door. It made a great picture – a sad lonely bear in the mud. That's how they do it.

Soon local people arrived and demanded that this 'evil child-killer' be taken away. They didn't want her near their children. The next day the police and social services arrived and took Robbie away. For his safety, they said. Carol hadn't told anyone that she'd got a son. She'd managed to hide away from the police and social services. She'd got a new identity and had started a new life on her own. And, until I arrived, she'd been doing very well.

She left a few days later. And so I never saw her again.

I resigned from the *Student News*. I knew I was never going to be a reporter. I never wanted to write for a newspaper again. I decided to become a teacher and go abroad. I wanted to go away, as far away from England as possible.

It all happened two years ago and today, although I live eight thousand kilometres from England, I am still back there. I can remember Carol's face as she watched Robbie finally find a circle and drop it through the circle-shaped hole. I remember that moment of happiness between them, and I can hear her screaming as they took Robbie away.

You see the thing is, when Angela rang the tabloids, they already knew about Carol. Because I had already emailed them. I had to get the story in first, didn't I? I was the star reporter.

Don't Miss the Mozart!

The train curled into the station, bending like a snake to reach the long platform; inside, the travellers standing near the exits grabbed hold of the seats to stop themselves from falling. Nicole Leconte looked at her watch. The train was on time. Good, she thought, she would have plenty of time to look around before her talk.

She picked up her small travelling case and stepped off the train, looking for somewhere where she could buy a map of the town. Or was it a city? It was the first time she had visited Norwich and she didn't know anything about the place.

The station was crowded; people getting off the train mixed with those waiting for their family and friends. Nicole tried to keep to one side and found herself in front of a large poster for the local football club. Norwich City it was called. 'Ah, so it's a city,' she reflected. One day, she decided, she really must get someone to tell her the difference.

There was a small shop selling newspapers and books, the kind you find in all English railway stations. Nicole was making her way there when she bumped into a young woman. Or rather, the young woman came flying through the door and ran straight into her.

'I'm so sorry,' the woman began. She was out of breath and had obviously been running.

The woman, Melanie, was about to run on when she

stopped and looked at the woman she had nearly knocked down.

Nicole was wearing a light brown raincoat, under which Melanie could see a black sweater and a black skirt. A silk scarf hung across her shoulders as if held there by magic. 'She must be French,' thought Melanie. 'Only a Frenchwoman could wear a scarf like that.' On her, she knew, it would instantly fall off. Melanie began to smile.

'Madame Leconte?' Nicole heard her ask, as if it was the most marvellous surprise to find her there, at that moment.

'Yes,' Nicole admitted. She was surprised that the university had sent someone to meet her. Usually she had to look after herself and if she was offered supper after her talk, she considered herself lucky. This was obviously going to be a good day.

'Thank goodness!' said Melanie. 'I'm so sorry I'm late. The traffic is awful; it just gets worse and worse all the time.' She spoke very quickly and Nicole, although she spoke very good English, found it hard to follow her. Melanie then took a deep breath and smiled again.

'Welcome to Norwich,' she said. 'My name is Melanie, but everyone calls me Mel.'

'How very kind,' Nicole smiled. 'I didn't expect anyone to come and meet me at the station,' she said.

'Didn't the office tell you?' Mel frowned. 'Or your agent? Never mind, I'm here now. What do you want to do first, go to your hotel or have lunch?'

Nicole did not have an agent, but she supposed that some senior professors did have agents to handle their talks so Mel's comment did not seem surprising at the time. Nor had she booked a hotel. She supposed that she would probably stay with another professor. That was what usually happened these days. Hotels, she had been told, were too expensive.

'I didn't expect a hotel,' Nicole admitted. 'I thought I'd be staying in someone's house.'

'Not you,' replied Mel. She sounded shocked. 'You're a star, aren't you?'

Until this moment this was a feeling Nicole had kept to herself. To go around saying you were a star would not be appreciated in university circles, however many books you had published. Nicole was charmed.

'Not really a star,' she told Mel. 'Or only in my very small circle.'

'You're too modest,' Mel said. 'We're all really looking forward to this evening.'

'How very kind,' said Nicole. 'I will certainly do my best then.' Mel laughed as if this was a joke. 'So, hotel first?' she asked.

'Yes, please,' declared Nicole. She could have a quick shower, she thought, before her talk. What a treat.

Mel led Nicole out of the station. There was a hotel immediately opposite, on the other side of the road. People were eating at a restaurant overlooking the river. Nicole thought it looked delightful, quite French in fact.

'We've put you here,' Mel told her. 'Then it will be easy for you to catch your train tomorrow. Is that OK?' she added.

'Superb,' said Nicole, wondering how the university could afford such an expensive hotel and whether she should have asked for a larger fee. 'How very thoughtful.'

She noticed, as they went inside, that it was a four-star

hotel and offered a heated swimming pool as well as a comfortable room. The university obviously had more money than most these days. This was no tiny bed and breakfast place on a noisy main road, the kind she had stayed in so frequently and disliked intensely. In one, when she had been two minutes late for breakfast, they had refused to give her anything, even a cup of coffee.

'You're late!' the owner had told her. He had even laughed. 'Breakfast is from eight till nine.' She had laughed too, at the time. She thought he had been joking. But then she'd realised that he had no intention of giving her breakfast. Nicole could not understand why people like him ran hotels or guesthouses, or whatever it was the English called them. They obviously didn't like people. She tried to imagine a French hotel refusing a guest a cup of coffee, but failed. It wouldn't happen.

And yet Nicole had to admit that she had also stayed in some delightful small bed and breakfast places in Britain, some of them on farms. And although she found English food rather heavy – cooked English breakfasts, for example, that nobody seemed to eat any more except in hotels – the people who ran these little places were charming. She loved the way they had maps showing local walks and would tell her where she could find wild flowers growing.

Nevertheless, when you were travelling, the pleasures of a luxury hotel were hard to beat. And it was not what universities usually offered visiting professors giving talks on climate change. Nicole knew that the department of climate change at this university was very well respected and that its research facilities were excellent, but all the same she was surprised. And pleased.

Mel waited for Nicole in the bar. She was so relieved she had found her. It had been such a bad day until then. It had been such a bad week. First she had forgotten to give someone a telephone message and it had later turned out to be very important, and then she had got lost driving to the printers and was late getting back to the office. She felt that everyone had been shouting at her all week and she was thoroughly fed up. At least today she was doing something right. She had met Madame Conte and they were getting on really well. Everything was fine.

'We thought that you'd probably like some lunch before you come and look at the hall,' Mel told Nicole after she came back down showered and feeling fresh.

'The hall?' Nicole interrupted

'For a soundcheck,' said Mel. 'I expect you want some time to check how the sound is.' Mel took a piece of paper out of her pocket and studied it. 'The office thought that you would probably want to go through everything from about two or three till five. But we can give you more time if you want it.'

Nicole was very surprised. It was true that she liked to check that the microphone actually worked before her talk and, if she was using her computer, she liked to check that, too. But she had never been asked if she wanted to go through everything before.

'I don't need all that time,' Nicole told Mel. 'I like to be fresh. I just go on and do it. But a soundcheck would be very helpful, just to get a feeling for the size of the hall.'

'Oh, fine. We didn't know,' Mel said apologetically. 'I'd better tell the office.' She took a mobile phone out of her bag and tried to dial a number.

'Oh, no,' she muttered. 'My battery's dead; I forgot to charge it up last night.' She turned to Nicole and smiled. 'I'll tell them later.'

Both Nicole and Mel thoroughly enjoyed their lunch. The food was better than Mel could afford to eat on her salary and Nicole had not been expecting such hospitality.

'Tell me,' said Nicole, as they drank their coffees and Mel ate both the chocolates, 'what's the difference between a city and a town?'

'I think it's that cities have cathedrals,' said Mel, frowning slightly. 'And the queen is allowed to make other important towns into cities, too. Or rather governments do. The queen just signs the bit of paper. I don't think she does the choosing. She doesn't actually have any power really.'

'So what do you think of Charles?' Nicole asked. 'Do you think he will make a good king?'

'Maybe if we were all vegetables,' replied Mel. 'You know that Prince Charles is famous for talking to vegetables.' She laughed. 'No, I'm not interested in any of the royal family,' she added. 'I don't know anyone who is.'

'You're a republican then, like us, like the French.' Nicole smiled.

'I don't really care one way or the other,' said Mel. 'I wouldn't want a president like they have in the States. Is that what you have?'

'Yes,' Nicole told her. She had studied in England and visited the country many times since, so this lack of knowledge of European politics did not surprise her any more. Though she had to admit that all the young people she met were scientists and most of them had been studying nothing but maths and science for many years. She thought that the English education system was very limiting in this way, though it did produce many fine specialists.

'Are you a scientist?' she asked Mel.

Mel frowned. She couldn't see the connection between republicanism and science. 'No,' she said. 'I have a music degree.'

Nicole went to many concerts and was happy to talk about music. She had noticed a poster for a music festival currently running in Norwich and commented on the design, which was bright and colourful.

'I'm glad you like our poster,' said Mel.

'Yes. It looks like an interesting festival.'

'It is,' Mel replied. She opened her bag and gave Nicole a leaflet. 'Here's a programme for you.'

'How kind,' said Nicole, looking through it. There were events every evening, and lunchtime concerts as well. 'That's an interesting concert on right now,' she commented. 'I really like that piece.'

'Yes, I would have gone to see it if I hadn't come to meet you,' Mel told her.

Nicole was sorry that Mel had missed the concert.

'Well it's worth it just to meet you.' Mel smiled and went a bit red. 'Mind you,' she said, 'you're not at all what I expected.'

Nicole laughed. 'Aren't I?' she asked.

'No, I thought you'd be rather distant and serious. And you're younger than I thought, too.'

'I'm older than you think,' Nicole joked. 'It must be a good day.'

Nicole looked at the festival programme again. That evening one of the best pianists in France was to play. Louise Conte. Nicole had heard her a couple of times in Paris and she would have very much enjoyed to see her again. But the concert was on at the same time as her talk. Louise Conte was going to play a Mozart concerto which was one of her favourite pieces.

'I do love the Mozart Third,' she told Mel.

'So do I,' she said. 'I expect it will be the highlight of the festival.'

'I expect you're right,' said Nicole. 'Don't miss it!'

Mel laughed. 'I never thought that you'd be so funny.'

Nicole did not understand what the joke was, but she often found English humour difficult and did not say anything. Instead she asked if they could walk around for a bit and visit the city. She knew there was a cathedral. Its stone had come from Rouen, where Nicole had been born.

'Norwich has thirty-two old churches,' Mel told her.

'So many?' Nicole was amazed. 'Are they still used?'

'Well, not all as churches,' said Mel. 'Some of them are used as arts centres or galleries or for selling antiques; one is a theatre. But they're all still standing.'

'I had no idea that there was so much to see here.' Nicole was impressed. She thought she might come back for a holiday. 'You must love living here, then,' said Nicole.

'I've only just moved here,' Mel told her, 'so I can't really say. There isn't a lot to do. There are a few places to go and there are a few cinemas and clubs, but it's not as lively as Manchester. That's where I was at university. I'd like to get a job up north; I like it better there. It's much friendlier.'

They stopped in front of a blue door in an old narrow street. 'Oh, here we are,' Mel said.

'What's this?' Nicole asked.

'It's the festival office,' Mel answered. 'Come in.'

Nicole thought Mel might be going in to get herself a ticket for the concert. She still had plenty of time to get to the university, so she followed her in.

Inside the first room, lots of people were talking on phones and to each other. They all stopped talking as Mel came in and looked at her strangely. Before Mel could speak, a woman with red hair and a dark blue suit came out of the next room. She looked furious and began to shout the moment she saw Mel.

'Where have you been Mel? Who's this?' she demanded, pointing to Nicole.

Mel stopped smiling. 'It's Madame Conte,' she answered.

'No it isn't,' shouted the woman angrily. 'Louise Conte arrived several hours ago. When no-one met her at the station, she got back on the train and returned to London. She refuses to come back and play tonight. Do you understand? We've sold almost a thousand tickets for her concert and we don't have a pianist. Just because of you and your stupidity.' The woman turned to Nicole. 'Who are you?' she shouted.

'My name is Nicole Leconte,' she said. 'I can see there has been a mistake. I am a scientist. I am giving a talk tonight at the university. I thought that Mel knew that . . .'

'Mel knows nothing,' interrupted the woman. 'Mel has caused nothing but trouble ever since she arrived here. And as from this moment she is finished.' She turned to Mel. 'Clear your desk and get out. And you,' she turned to Nicole, 'can remove yourself from the hotel. I have three hours to find myself a world-famous pianist who is willing to get here and perform the Mozart.'

*   *   *

'And that was it,' Mel told her friends in Manchester some weeks later. They had heard the story before, but they were friends and knew Mel was still upset.

'Do you know what you say to a music graduate?' Mel asked them.

'No,' they replied. In fact they did know. Mel had often asked them this. It was an old joke, but they played along with her.

'No,' they all said. 'What do you say to a music graduate?'

'Two hamburgers and a coffee,' said Mel angrily.

'You're still working in the café, then?' asked one of her friends.

'Yes,' replied Mel, 'I am. I can't get a job in the music business because everyone knows everyone else. And now everyone knows the story of me and Madame Conte, no-one will give me a job.'

'That's not fair,' acknowledged another friend.

'It isn't,' complained Mel. 'And it's all the fault of Louise Conte. If she'd got a taxi to the office like any normal person, none of this would have happened. I blame her.

And that other stupid Frenchwoman, the scientist. She should have guessed. But if Louise Conte had played, I'd still have a job. I blame her,' she repeated.

'I read a bit about her in the paper today,' the same friend commented. 'She's playing at that big concert that Prince Charles has organised. She says she's really excited to have been asked. She's doing a Mozart concerto.'

'Really,' said Mel. 'Well I hope it rains all evening. I hope there's thunder and lightning and no-one can hear her playing.'

The following days it seemed that the papers couldn't write about anything else except this concert. People all over the world were going to watch it. Mel began to have an idea. And the more she thought about it, the better the idea seemed.

*   *   *

The day of the concert a large black car drove up outside the Dorchester Hotel in London. The driver, a young woman wearing a dark uniform, walked up to the desk.

'Can you tell Madame Louise Conte that her car has arrived,' said the driver.

'Certainly,' said the man behind the desk. He picked up a telephone.

Louise Conte did not seem surprised that a car had been sent to pick her up. She didn't look at the female driver who held the door open for her. 'It's a fine day,' she said as they drove out of the capital and along the motorway. She studied her music and did not notice the road signs saying they were heading north instead of south to Salisbury, where the concert was to take place.

'Yes,' replied Mel, driving smoothly along in the car she had hired the previous day. 'It's a lovely day,' she said silently to herself. 'Just the day for a long drive into the country.'

The Shivering Mountain

It was raining again. It rained every day.

'Only a shower,' Nick's father would say. 'Nothing to worry about.' And the family would agree, even Nick, and they would walk on laughing and talking to each other while Paolo followed after them, the rain hitting his face and running down the back of his neck.

This was the worst holiday of his life, Paolo decided. He was staying for three weeks with Nick and his family. The first week hadn't been too bad. He and Nick had gone out to the local cinema a couple of times to see the latest films, and they'd been up to London.

'I'm sitting in a café in a district called Covent Garden,' he wrote on a postcard to his best friend at home. 'You'd like it here. It's more like Italy than England, lots of cafés and bars and shops. Really international, too. Especially the birds, which is what Nick calls the girls. I wish we could spend more time in London, but the family is going on holiday to somewhere called the Peak District. It doesn't sound very promising. Love to all.'

The Peak District was worse than he'd feared, Paolo decided. He hated it. He hated everything about the place.

'It's in Derbyshire, Paolo,' Nick's father, Mr Fowler, had explained last year when the holiday had been discussed with Paolo and his parents. 'I'm not sure why it's called the Peak District. There aren't any real peaks. I think the name must have something to do with the people who used to live there.'

Mr Fowler was an English teacher; he loved explaining things. If you asked him a question, he would always go to a dictionary and tell you not only the answer itself, but the reason why that was the answer. Nick always groaned when his father took the dictionary off the shelf.

'Just tell us the word, Dad.' he would say. 'Dictionaries are so boring.'

Paolo agreed with Nick. He couldn't understand how anyone could enjoy looking up words all the time. Until now Paolo had considered that he and Nick agreed on most things. The previous year Nick had stayed with him and his family in Pisa and they had had a good time together.

Paolo's mother was a teacher, too, and Nick had arrived with a pile of books that his father had thought she would enjoy. Paolo, in turn, had brought a variety of Italian books on English literature on this trip. The parents now emailed each other and got on very well.

No, thought Paolo. There was nothing he could do. If he rang his parents and said he wanted to go home, they wouldn't listen. They would just laugh and tell him that it was good for him to experience English life and English weather.

'If you want to go to university next year,' his father had told him, 'it's very important to be able to speak English well. And the best way to learn that, apart from reading, is by going to England and living with a family. You're lucky that you know Nick, and that his parents are willing to let you stay for three weeks.'

'Of course the one thing we're all mad about,' Mr Fowler had told Paolo before they left London, 'is bird-watching.'

Paolo expected Nick to either groan or make a joke about birds in short skirts. But he didn't.

'Yeah,' Nick agreed happily. 'We saw a sparrowhawk last year just above this valley. It was really beautiful.'

'You don't really enjoy going out and looking at birds, do you?' asked Paolo, horrified.

Nick blushed. 'Well, actually I do. I mean we've done it all our lives. Now it's just part of the summer holidays. And hawks are really amazing to watch. There are goshawks in the Peaks, but I've never seen one yet.'

Paolo was disgusted. Bird-watching! This was going to be the worst two weeks of his life.

'The Fowlers walk in the rain, which never stops,' Paolo wrote to his parents. 'They look at birds through binoculars, then they write down the names of the birds they see. Next week they are planning a long walk up to a peak called Bleaklow – which describes my holiday. It's cold, it's wet and I'm feeling low. I hope you're having a great time. Paolo.'

His parents had a holiday home in Marina di Cecina, by the sea. He thought of the heat and the smell of the pine trees outside and the pleasure of hot sand under his feet. He couldn't imagine being warm and dry again. Even his socks were damp.

And now here he was walking up a dark hill, which went on for ever, on a dark day when it seemed that it would never stop raining. It wasn't raining hard, but it was wet and horrible.

'Soft rain, they call it in Ireland,' Mr Fowler told him cheerfully.

'What does it matter what they call it?' thought Paolo as he felt his clothes getting heavier and heavier as they got wetter and wetter. It was like being inside a cloud, he decided. You couldn't escape it. As you walked in it, you just got wetter and wetter and bigger and bigger. In the end you'd look like a sheep. There was nothing but sheep all around them.

Paolo was glad that none of his friends could see him. The clothes, for a start, would make them laugh till they were sick. He was wearing a bright blue outdoor jacket they called an anorak, and a pair of thick socks inside his new walking boots.

'I talked to your mother and she said that we should buy you a pair of proper boots,' Mrs Fowler had said.

'Can't I just wear trainers?' asked Paolo.

'You can't walk properly in trainers, can you Nick?' And Nick, his friend Nick, who usually took his side against adult stupidities, had agreed with his mother.

'No,' Nick had told Paolo. 'You really do need boots for walking. The stones are often slippery in the wet and trainers are dangerous then.' Paolo had not liked the sound of that description, but he had allowed Mrs Fowler to take him shopping for walking boots.

They had gone into a special outdoor shop which sold tents and things to put inside tents and a variety of things Paolo had never seen before but that seemed to be connected with camping. At least he would be spared the horror of sleeping in a tent; the Fowlers had rented a cottage. If Nick took his computer games, perhaps it would not be too bad.

Nick's younger sister Lucy came with them on the shopping trip. She had a way of picking out the most expensive item in every shop. It amused Paolo, who thought that she showed good taste, but her mother was getting increasingly annoyed.

'How about one of these jackets?' Lucy asked.

The jackets were dark green and, said Lucy, they were waxed. When Paolo felt them, they had the shiny sticky feel of a candle. They weren't too bad, he thought. He'd seen people wear them at home.

'Don't be ridiculous, Lucy!' complained Mrs Fowler. 'Have you looked at how much they cost?'

Lucy looked at the price. 'Oh,' she said. 'Why are they so expensive?' she asked her mother.

'I don't know,' her mother replied. 'They just are. Now if you can't be more helpful, Lucy, then just be quiet. I think an anorak like this will do,' she said, handing him something horribly bright. 'It will keep out the wind and the rain.'

Paolo allowed her to put it on him, although he thought it was the ugliest bit of clothing he had ever seen. Even if they bought it, he had made up his mind that he was never, ever going to wear it.

'And I expect it will be quite useful at home in the winter,' Mrs Fowler added.

Paolo imagined himself wearing the anorak back at home and shook his head. He'd rather walk round the piazza naked than let anyone see him in that anorak.

But now, here he was in the rain on a black hill in this same horrible blue anorak. The Fowlers didn't seem to care what they looked like. Even Nick, who normally wouldn't wear anything unless it had a designer label, wore an old red anorak and walking boots.

Nick had been behaving very differently ever since they left London. He didn't seem to mind that the cottage they had rented was cold and smelt.

'It's just damp,' he told Paolo. 'It's because the cottage is empty so much. The smell goes away after a bit.'

Nick laughed at Paolo's disgusted expression. He seemed to enjoy the fact that Paolo disliked everything about the country. The more things Paolo complained about, the more Nick laughed. It was as if he had become a different person in the country. Nick didn't seem to mind the rain and just said it was always like that. Nick didn't mind the lack of television, or cinemas or cafés or any of the things that Paolo had always thought were an essential part of life.

In fact Nick seemed to get more and more cheerful every day. 'Look!' he exclaimed on a walk one afternoon. 'There's Mam Tor! They say if you can see Mam Tor, that means it's going to rain.'

'And if you can't see it?'

'That's because it's already raining.' Nick seemed to think this was funny for some reason. Paolo was beginning to ask himself what it was about Nick that he'd once liked. 'The Tor's also called the Shivering Mountain,' Nick explained. 'But of course it's not a mountain, just a hill. It's a great walk,' he added.

Paolo had heard this last piece of information before, on the journey to the cottage. Paolo hadn't enjoyed the drive north from London. Mrs Fowler had commented on everyone else's driving all the time.

'Look at that car, the speed he's doing! Did you see the way he cut in front of me?'

Mr Fowler never replied, but made noises of disapproval.

'The cottage is near the village of Castleton, near Mam Tor,' Nick said. Paolo hadn't asked Nick why Mam Tor was called the Shivering Mountain. He knew that Mr Fowler would have a long explanation.

'There are lots of words in English that aren't what they seem to be,' Paolo said instead. 'Like the main street in every town is called the high street, but it isn't high.'

Mr Fowler laughed. 'Yes,' he began, 'but that's because the word high . . .'

'Oh Dad!' interrupted Nick. 'Really! Paolo isn't interested in why a high street is called . . .'

'I'm sure he is,' argued Mr Fowler. 'That's why he mentioned it.'

'And you say you're going down to the country but you're driving north,' continued Paolo, who had been puzzling over this expression for some days.

Mr Fowler was about to tell everyone the reason for this expression when his wife protested so loudly that everyone jumped. A car coming in the other direction had started to overtake a lorry and Mrs Fowler had to brake hard to avoid hitting it.

'Did you see that?' she screamed. 'The madman! He could have killed the lot of us!' And that brought the conversation to an end.

Hours later – they had stopped for tea at a motorway café which Mrs Fowler said was disgusting and ridiculously expensive – they arrived at the cottage. The cottage was made of grey stone and sat in the middle of a deep valley. The valley, Paolo noted, was grey too. And so was the sky. Paolo thought of the blue summer skies of home and imagined all his friends having their annual holidays by the sea, swimming and playing football on the beach. By the time he got home the summer holidays would be almost over and he would start the term as the only boy in the school who didn't have a suntan. He'd look like a foreigner. It wasn't surprising that the English went crazy when they went to Italy. Everyone laughed at them because all they did was lie in the sun, even during the hottest midday hours when everyone else was having a siesta. But after a few days of an English summer Paolo could understand them.

The cottage was bad enough and the weather was worse, but the thing that really annoyed Paolo was how Nick had changed. It wasn't just that he seemed to enjoy all the things that Paolo hated, but at home in London he was always arguing with his parents. Here it seemed as if he actually agreed with them. And he hadn't brought his computer games.

'Not really worth it,' he told Paolo. 'We're outside most of the time; there's so much to do here.'

Paolo looked out at the misty landscape and couldn't think of anything he wanted to do there except leave.

But Nick and his father were already looking at maps and planning the next day's walk. Paolo had never thought about maps and guidebooks before, but here it seemed they were essential. And it seemed to matter, too, that you had the right ones. There was a guidebook on churches that had been written by someone called Pevsner, and they could not leave the house without Pevsner.

'Is Pevsner in the car?' Mrs Fowler would call, and Paolo had the quick impression of a tired old man sitting in the car waiting for them. Every time they drove through a new village, Mrs Fowler would read out what Pevsner said about the church or some other building there. Paolo didn't understand a word.

Nick had tried once or twice to show Paolo why maps were so interesting. 'Look, just here,' he explained, pointing to some circular lines. 'This is where we're going tomorrow. You can see by these lines just how steep it is. And you can see that there's a wood over there and down there's the river.'

'You can see that when you get there,' replied Paolo. 'So what's the point?'

'The point is . . . Oh, if you aren't interested, I can't tell you.' Nick put the map away.

'So what will we see tomorrow?' asked Paolo.

'Lots of birds, maybe some hawks if we're lucky. And lots of wild animals.'

'Are they safe?' asked Paolo.

'Oh yes, the sheep only killed a couple of people last year,' Nick told him happily.

'Don't take any notice of Nick,' said Lucy, who had just walked into the room. 'It's just one of his bad jokes. The sheep don't hurt anyone. The only dangerous thing here is the mist. You can get lost if you walk in the mist and take a wrong turning and fall. But mummy and daddy never let us walk on the hills when the mist is bad.'

Paolo had never noticed Lucy much in London; she was just Nick's little sister. But here he began to like her. She walked more slowly than the rest of her family and stayed with him, while Nick walked ahead with his father. And she told him lots of stories about the area.

'You see that road there between those two cliffs,' she said one afternoon as she and Paolo followed the family out of the village of Castleton. 'It's called Winnats Pass and it's haunted.'

'Haunted?'

'Yes,' Lucy continued. 'Haunted; you know, with ghosts. The story is that there was a boy and girl from two families who were enemies and they ran away together one winter night. And it got very cold and began to snow and they were trapped between the cliffs and couldn't get out. The villagers found them months later when the snow melted; they'd died in each other's arms. They say you can still hear them calling out on the mountain.'

'What rubbish is my sister telling you now?' asked Nick, who had walked back.

'Nothing,' said Paolo. 'Just local history.'

'Well if she didn't talk so much, she might be able to walk a bit faster. Do come on, you two; we've got a long way to go today.'

'You go then,' said Paolo, furious. 'I'm going back to Castleton.'

'Why don't you get the train to Sheffield?' Nick asked. 'You obviously don't enjoy the country.' Paolo noticed that when Nick got angry, the back of his neck went bright red.

'Well maybe I'll do just that!' Paolo replied, and turned round and walked back along the road to the village.

By the time Paolo found out the times of the trains it was too late to get one that day, so he spent the rest of the day walking round the village of Castleton. There were jewellery shops selling things made of the local blue stone called Blue John and a shop selling anoraks and boots. At home, he thought, there would be a square with cafés and people sitting and talking and drinking coffee. Here everything was designed to make you walk. Even the shop selling chocolates also sold maps. Everyone went there in order to find out how to get somewhere else. There were lots of tourists in the village and they all seemed happy. They visited the castle and the caves.

Paolo thought that he might visit the Peak Cavern. There was a riverside path which went up between some old miners' cottages into a huge steep valley. Looking up, he could see Peveril Castle, right above him. He remembered how Nick had warned him to be careful when they were exploring the castle. Now he could understand why.

The cave entrance was extraordinary. It was inside the high vertical cliffs and the entrance was bigger than any cathedral Paolo had ever visited. There was a guide taking a party of tourists round and Paolo joined them. He found that his English was good enough to understand almost everything that was said.

Peak Cavern, the guide told the group, was the biggest natural cave in Derbyshire and also had the largest entrance to any cave in Britain. In fact, the village of Castleton was once situated inside it. The village was built by rope makers who carried on their work in the entrance for over four hundred years. People said of the village that it was where the sun never shone and the rain never fell. The guide also said that local people thought the Devil lived in the cave and that the underground river was the River Styx which led to the world of the dead.

Paolo thought that he'd read that the River Styx was in Greece, but he didn't argue. It was a huge cave. On a good day he would have enjoyed it. He and Nick could have pretended to get lost, and frightened Lucy. But on his own it didn't seem the same. After a bit he left and went back to the cottage.

The Fowlers, even Lucy, seemed disappointed that he hadn't gone with them and only wanted to talk about what they'd seen on the walk and where they were going the next day. They didn't seem particularly interested in Paolo's visit to the cavern. Paolo left them talking and went to bed early. But he slept badly and when he woke up it was only five in the morning. He knew that he wasn't going to be able to get back to sleep, so he got dressed and went outside. There was a faint mist as he set off past the cavern to the end of the road. A path on the right led down to a farm. Paolo could hear a dog barking in the distance. He turned left and started climbing up past a row of cottages towards Mam Tor.

After a bit, the road became a path and it wasn't a grassy path but made of small stones. Paolo was glad that he was wearing his boots. It was quite difficult to walk on the stones, they kept slipping under his feet. The mist was quite thick in places, but he could just see the top of the mountain above him.

He kept on climbing slowly until, just as he reached the top of the mountain, he heard a voice calling out. 'Someone's fallen,' he thought; 'I must find them.'

'Hello!' he called.

The voice replied, but he couldn't hear what it said.

'Hello!' he called again. 'Hello! Where are you?'

He walked towards where the sound was coming from. Now it was almost as if there were two voices calling out to each other, a boy and a girl. They sounded despairing.

Paolo stepped forwards. He had one foot over the edge when he was grabbed from behind and thrown down on to the path.

'Ow!' complained Paolo. 'What on earth!'

'One second later . . . just one second later and . . .'

Paolo looked up and Nick was standing there. 'You fool, you crazy Italian fool!' Nick shouted. 'Couldn't you see where you were going?'

Paolo raised himself up on to his knees and looked down. There was nothing there, just a vertical drop down to the valley. He went white. 'One second later,' he thought, 'one second later and I'd have gone down there.'

'I thought I heard voices,' he began.

'What voices?' asked Nick.

'I don't know,' said Paolo. 'They came from down there . . .' He pointed below, but as he did so, the mist began to clear and he could see there was no-one anywhere near. As Paolo looked around, the sun rose above the hills away in the east and the fields below turned green and purple in the early morning light.

'I . . .' Paolo began, but as he spoke, he and Nick saw a large bird fly over their heads. It stopped right above them and then let the air carry it high across the valley.

'A goshawk,' murmured Nick.

'It's amazing,' said Paolo. He watched the bird and for the first time understood why his friend Nick loved coming

110

here to these strange and beautiful hills. And he knew two other things. One was that he and Nick would be friends for the rest of their lives. The second was that neither of them would tell anyone else about how Paolo had so nearly died that day, up on the Shivering Mountain.

Cambridge English Readers

Other titles available at Level 6:

Trumpet Voluntary
by Jeremy Harmer

A musician disappears. Her husband sets out to find her and begins a journey that takes him back into their shared past and forward to a future he had never dreamed about. This is a thriller set all around the world and deep into the human heart.

Deadly Harvest
by Carolyn Walker

Jane Honeywell is a city detective living in a sleepy country town. The peace and quiet is suddenly disturbed by a horrible murder and Jane starts the dangerous pursuit of the killer, or killers.

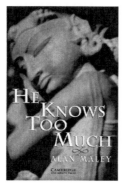

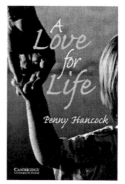

He Knows too Much
by Alan Maley

An English company executive in India is dismissed after he tries to unveil corruption within his company. He sets out on a quest for the truth behind his dismissal.

A Love for Life
by Penny Hancock

Fanella faces the challenge of adopting a child alone after her partner leaves her. Then Rod, a teacher who has problems of his own, comes into her life. Fanella has difficult choices and exciting discoveries to make.